HOW TO TURN INVISIBLE
AND OTHER SPELLS FOR KIDS

STELLA ROSE

Copyright Stella Rose 2023
All rights reserved.
www.stellawilkinson.com/stella-rose

This Book of Spells Belongs To

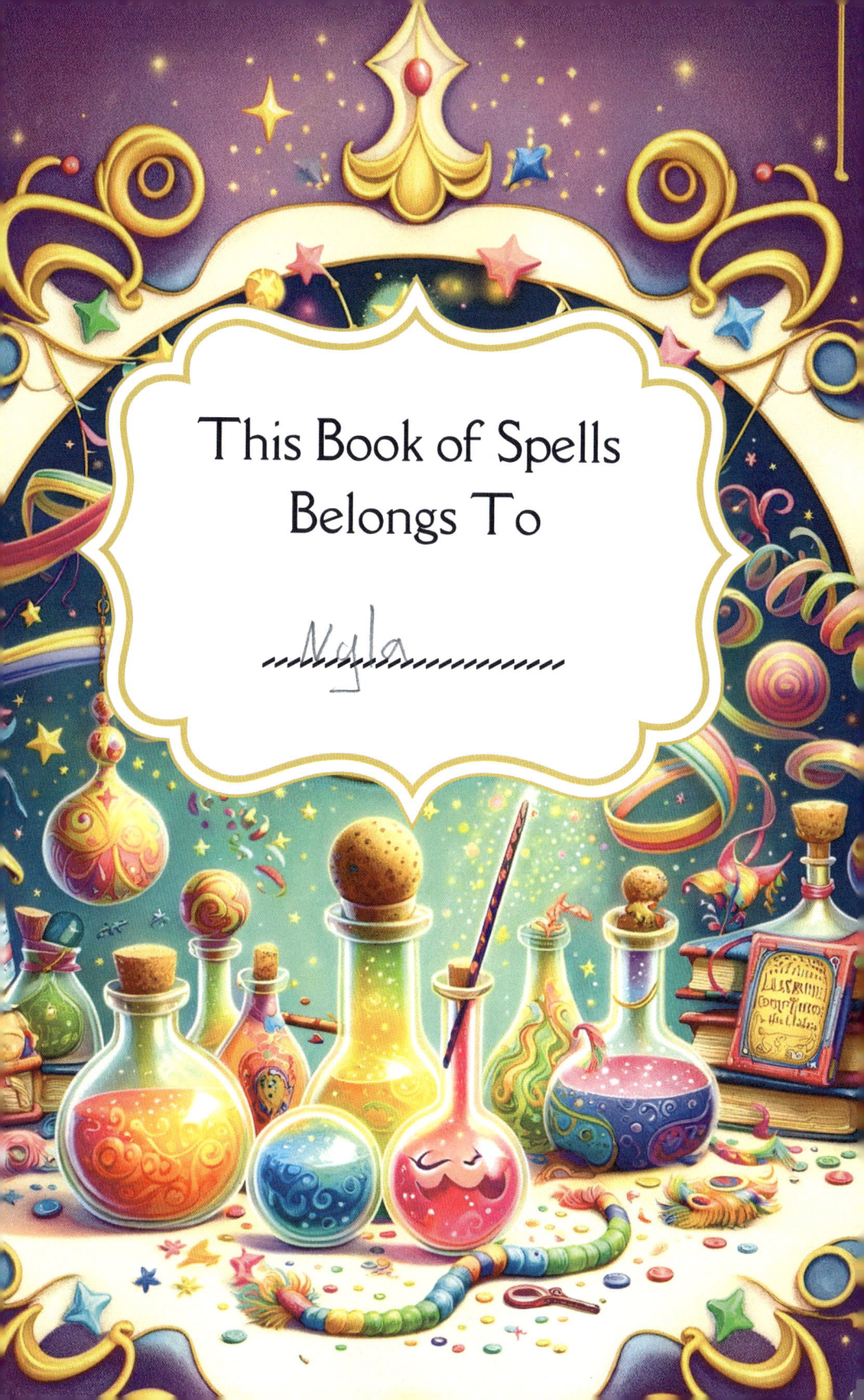

Nyla

Dedication:

For Jasper & Rose
Love Mum

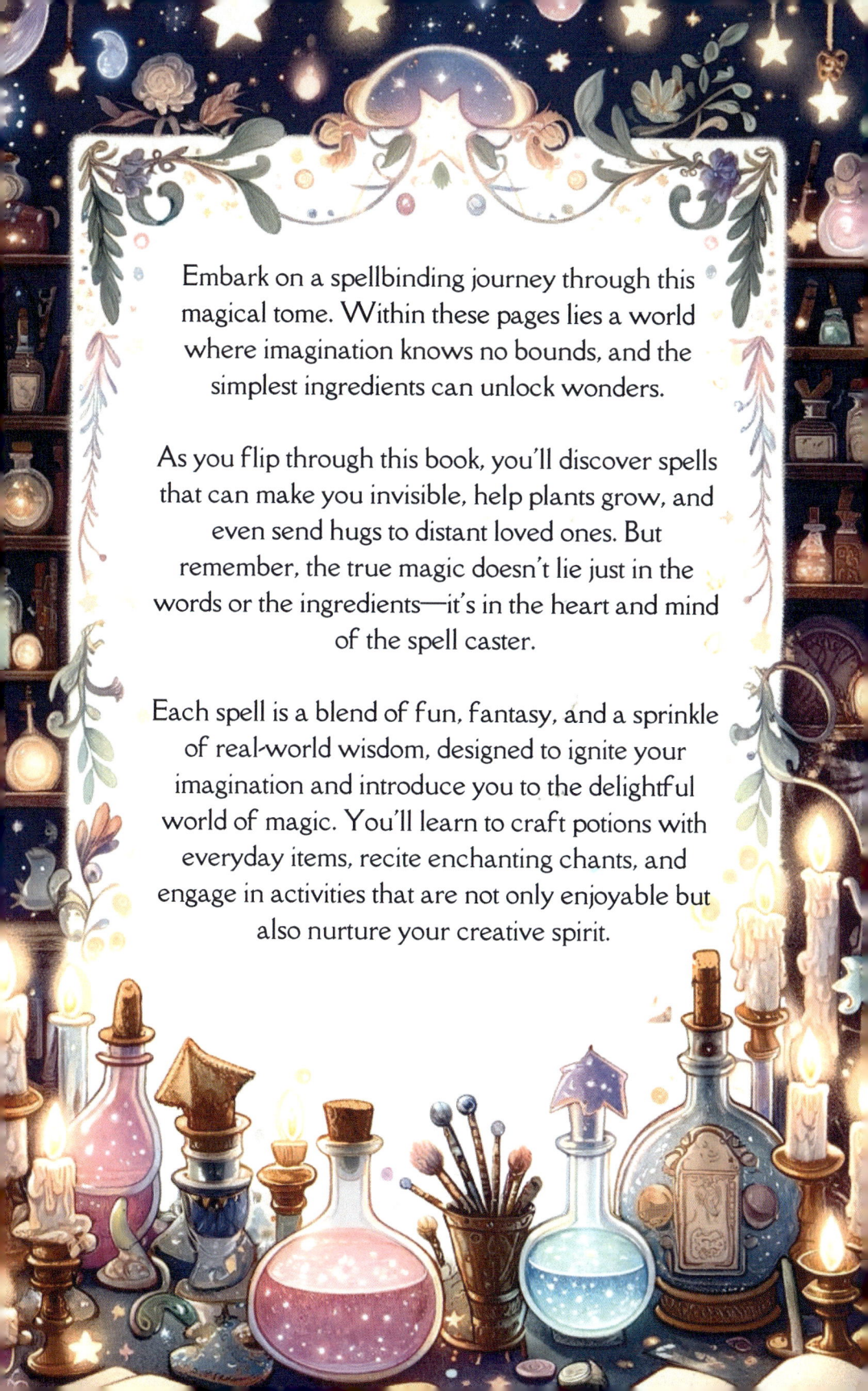

Embark on a spellbinding journey through this magical tome. Within these pages lies a world where imagination knows no bounds, and the simplest ingredients can unlock wonders.

As you flip through this book, you'll discover spells that can make you invisible, help plants grow, and even send hugs to distant loved ones. But remember, the true magic doesn't lie just in the words or the ingredients—it's in the heart and mind of the spell caster.

Each spell is a blend of fun, fantasy, and a sprinkle of real-world wisdom, designed to ignite your imagination and introduce you to the delightful world of magic. You'll learn to craft potions with everyday items, recite enchanting chants, and engage in activities that are not only enjoyable but also nurture your creative spirit.

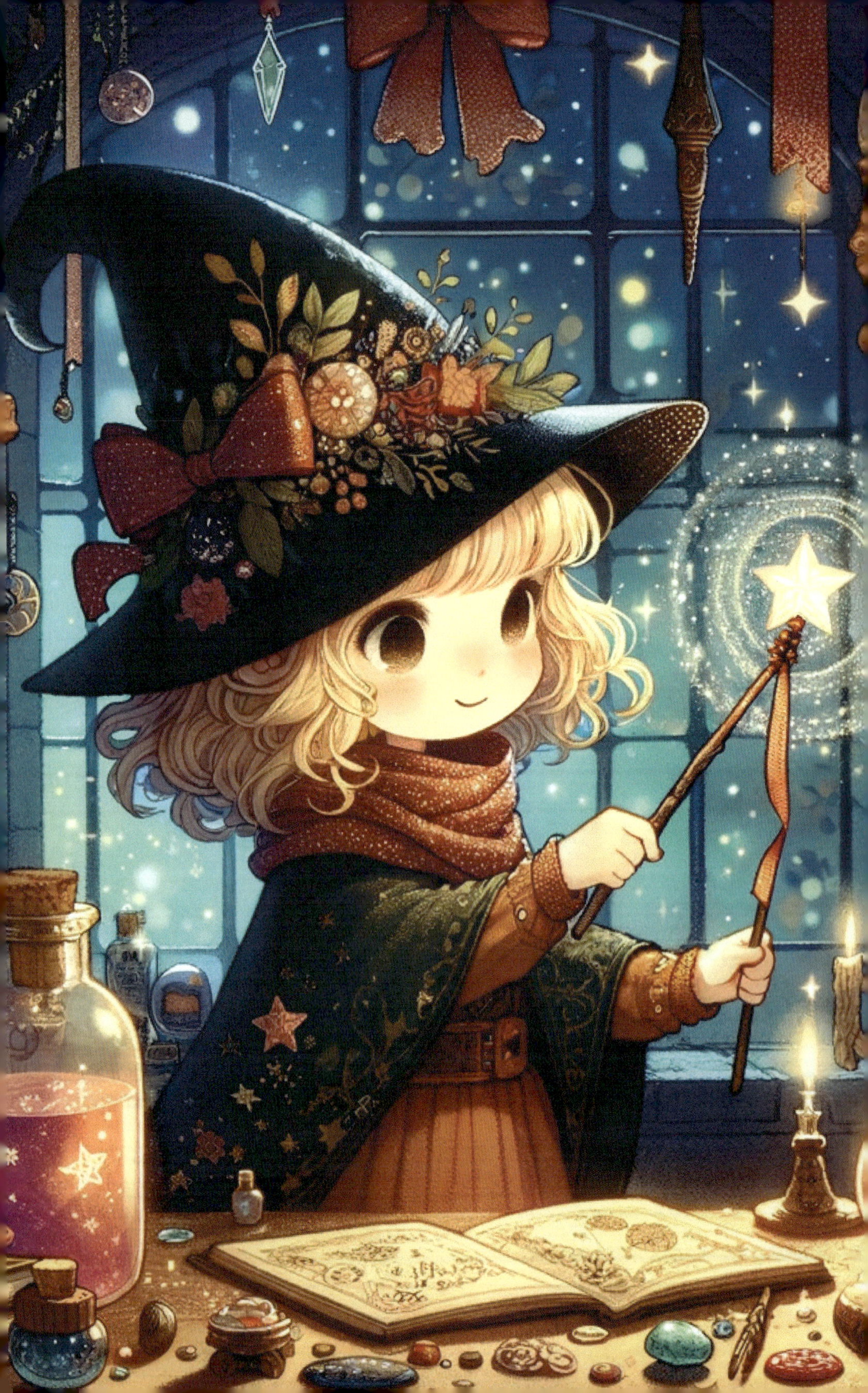

Wand Enchantment Spell

Purpose: To transform a simple stick into a wand brimming with magical potential.

Magical Ingredients:
- A Stick - Choose one that feels right in your hand, about the length of your forearm.
- Colorful Ribbons or Strings - To imbue the wand with vibrancy and power.
- Small Shiny Stones or Sequins - To add a sparkle of magic.
- A Clear Quartz Crystal - For amplifying your magical intentions (optional).

Directions:
- Prepare Your Space: Find a quiet place where you can concentrate and be creative. Lay out your materials.
- Decorate the Stick: Carefully tie the ribbons or strings around the stick. You can also attach small shiny stones or sequins to the wand with non-toxic glue for extra sparkle.
- Place the Crystal: If you have a clear quartz crystal, affix it to the top of the wand. This crystal will serve as the source of your wand's power.
- Recite the Chant: Hold your almost-complete wand in your hands, close your eyes, and recite the magical chant:

> "Stick of wood, plain and small,
> Transform now, at magic's call.
> Ribbons, stones, and crystal light,
> Become my wand, with power bright."

- Final Touches: Wave your wand gently in the air, imagining it filling with magical energy and light.
- Believe in the Magic: Feel the transformation from a simple stick to a wand of power. Remember, the true magic lies in your imagination and belief.
- Use Wisely: Use your new wand for good deeds, creative play, and to spread positivity wherever you go.

Magical Note: This enchanting process turns a mundane object into a special tool of imagination. It's a reminder that with creativity and belief, anything can be magical.

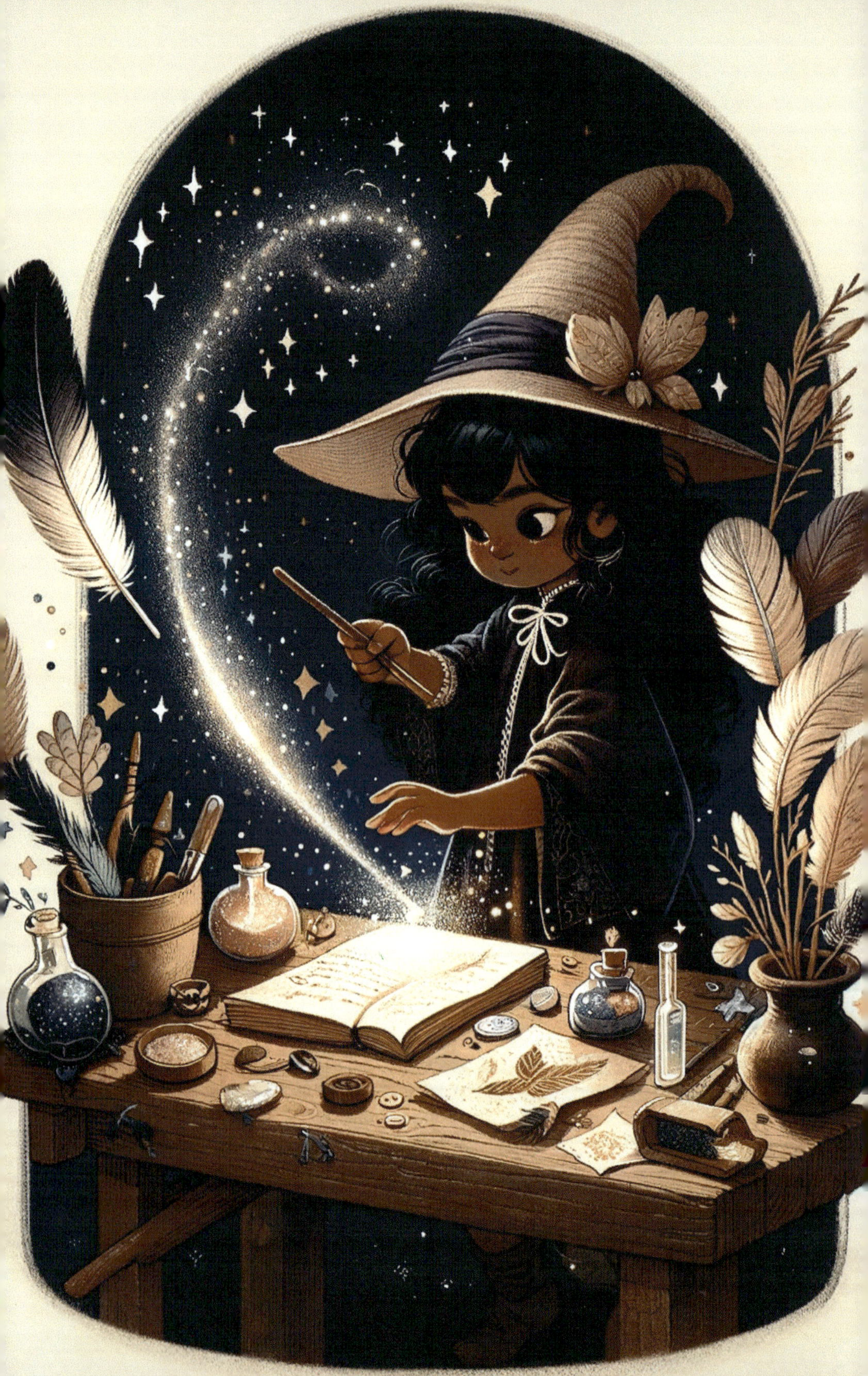

Invisibility Spell

Purpose: To make yourself invisible to the eyes of others.

Magical Ingredients:

- A Sheet of Paper - Represents the thin veil between being seen and unseen.
- A Feather - Symbolizes lightness and the ability to float away from sight.
- Eco-Friendly Glitter - To add a magical shimmer to your spell.
- Magic Wand - A tool to direct your magical energy.
- Potion Ingredients:

  A pinch of sugar (for sweetness and lightness)
  Three drops of lemon juice (for clarity and brightness)
  A cup of water (as a base for your potion)

Directions

Prepare Your Space: Find a quiet corner where you can focus without interruptions. Lay your sheet of paper on the ground.

Feather and Glitter: Place the feather on the paper and sprinkle some eco-friendly glitter around it. This creates your magical area.

Mix the Potion: In your cup, mix together the sugar, lemon juice, and water. Stir with your magic wand, channeling your energy into the potion.

Recite the Chant: Holding your magic wand, stand over the paper and feather. Recite the magical chant:

> "Feather light and paper sheer,
> Make me vanish, disappear.
> Potion stir, with magic bind,
> Invisibility I find."

Drink the Potion: Gently sip the potion, imagining each sip cloaking you in invisibility.

Visualization: Close your eyes and visualize yourself becoming as light as the feather, transparent and blending into your surroundings.

Believe in Magic: Remember, the true power of this spell lies in your imagination. Believe in your magic, and feel yourself fading from view.

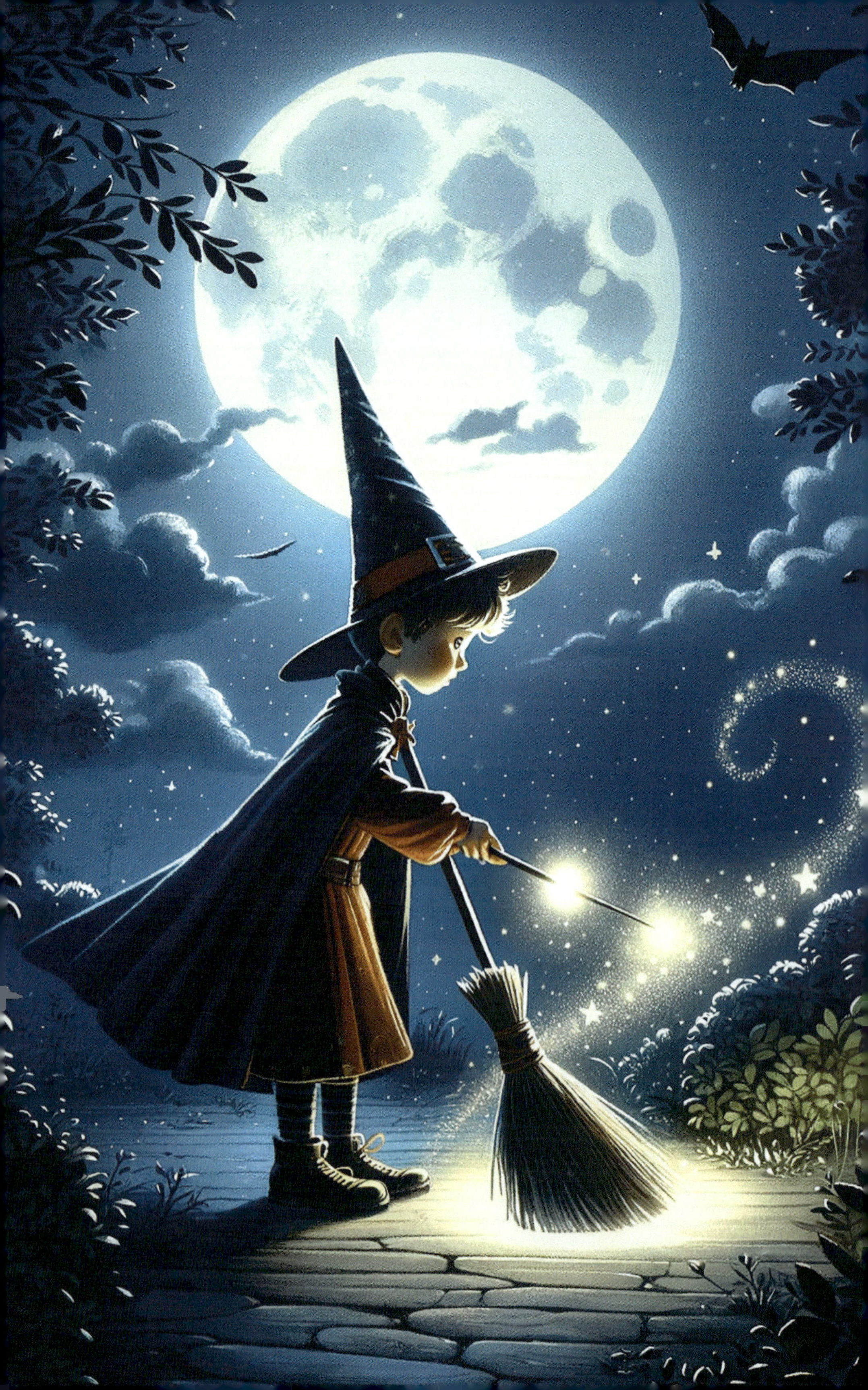

Broomstick Flight Spell

Purpose: To imagine soaring through the sky on a magical broomstick.

Magical Ingredients:

- A Broomstick - Your vehicle for magical flight.
- A Silk Scarf or Ribbon - Represents the wind and freedom of flight.
- A Handful of Leaves - Symbolizes the connection with the air and trees.

Directions:

- Prepare Your Space: Find a safe, open area where you can move freely without obstacles. This can be indoors or outdoors.
- Decorate the Broomstick: Tie the silk scarf or ribbon near the top of the broomstick handle, letting it flutter freely like a flag.
- Scatter the Leaves: Gently scatter the leaves around the base of your broomstick, creating a circle of nature's magic.
- Recite the Chant: Stand beside your broomstick, place one hand on it, and with a spirit of excitement, recite the magical chant:

> "Broom of wood and wind so free,
> Soar through sky, just you and me.
> Leaves that flutter, take us high,
> Glide and swoop through the open sky."

- Activate Your Imagination: Close your eyes and visualize yourself lifting off the ground, soaring through the air on your magical broomstick.
- Enjoy the Ride: While keeping your feet safely on the ground, run around your space, broomstick in hand, feeling the wind in your hair and the joy of flight.
- Land Safely: When you're ready to land, slow down and gently bring your broomstick back to the starting point, thanking it for the magical journey.

Magical Note: This spell is all about imagination and the joy of pretending. While we can't really fly on broomsticks, the magic of play and imagination can take us anywhere!

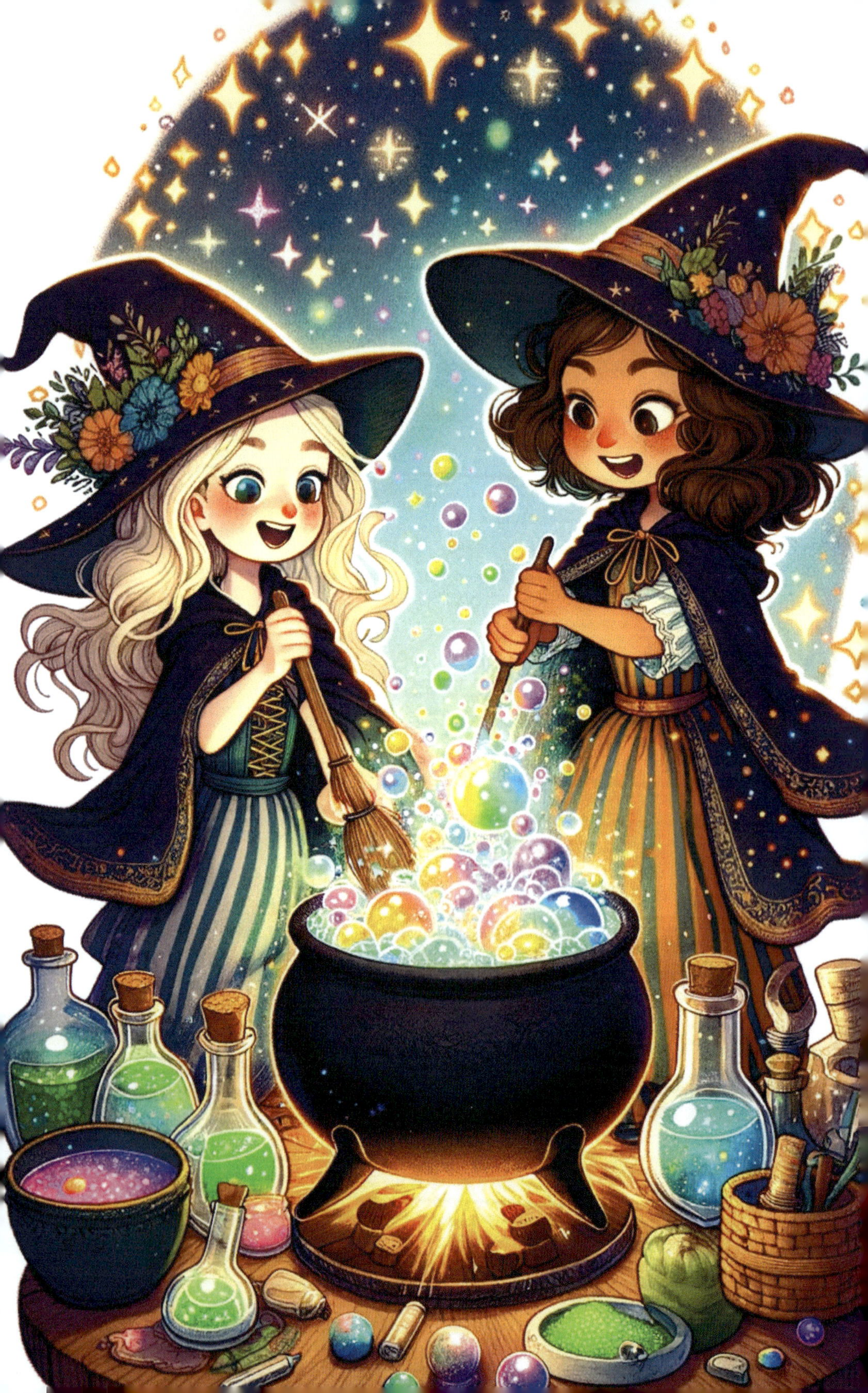

Laughter Potion

Purpose: To bring forth joy and laughter.

Magical Ingredients:

- A Spoonful of Sugar - For sweetness and joy.
- A Slice of Banana - To add a smile and light-heartedness.
- A Sprinkle of Cinnamon - For a spark of fun.
- Magic Wand - To mix and empower your potion.
- Eco-Friendly Confetti - To add a burst of happiness.

Directions:
- Prepare Your Space: Find a comfortable spot where laughter is welcome. Lay out your ingredients with joy.
- Mix the Potion: In a bowl, mix the spoonful of sugar, the slice of banana, and the sprinkle of cinnamon. Use your magic wand to stir, infusing the potion with giggles and grins.
- Confetti Magic: Scatter eco-friendly confetti around your bowl, symbolizing bursts of laughter.
- Recite the Chant: With your magic wand in hand, recite the chant with a smile:

    "Sugar sweet and banana peel,
    Bring forth laughter, joy we'll feel.
    Cinnamon dash, let it mix,
    Giggles and chuckles, this potion fix."

- Drink the Potion: Gently sip your laughter potion, feeling joy bubbling up inside you.
- Feel the Joy: Allow the laughter to flow naturally. Imagine each sip tickling your taste buds and bringing a smile to your face.
- Spread the Happiness: Share your joy with those around you. Remember, laughter is contagious!

Magical Note: This potion is a delightful way to encourage happiness and laughter. It's a celebration of joy, perfect for sharing with friends and family.

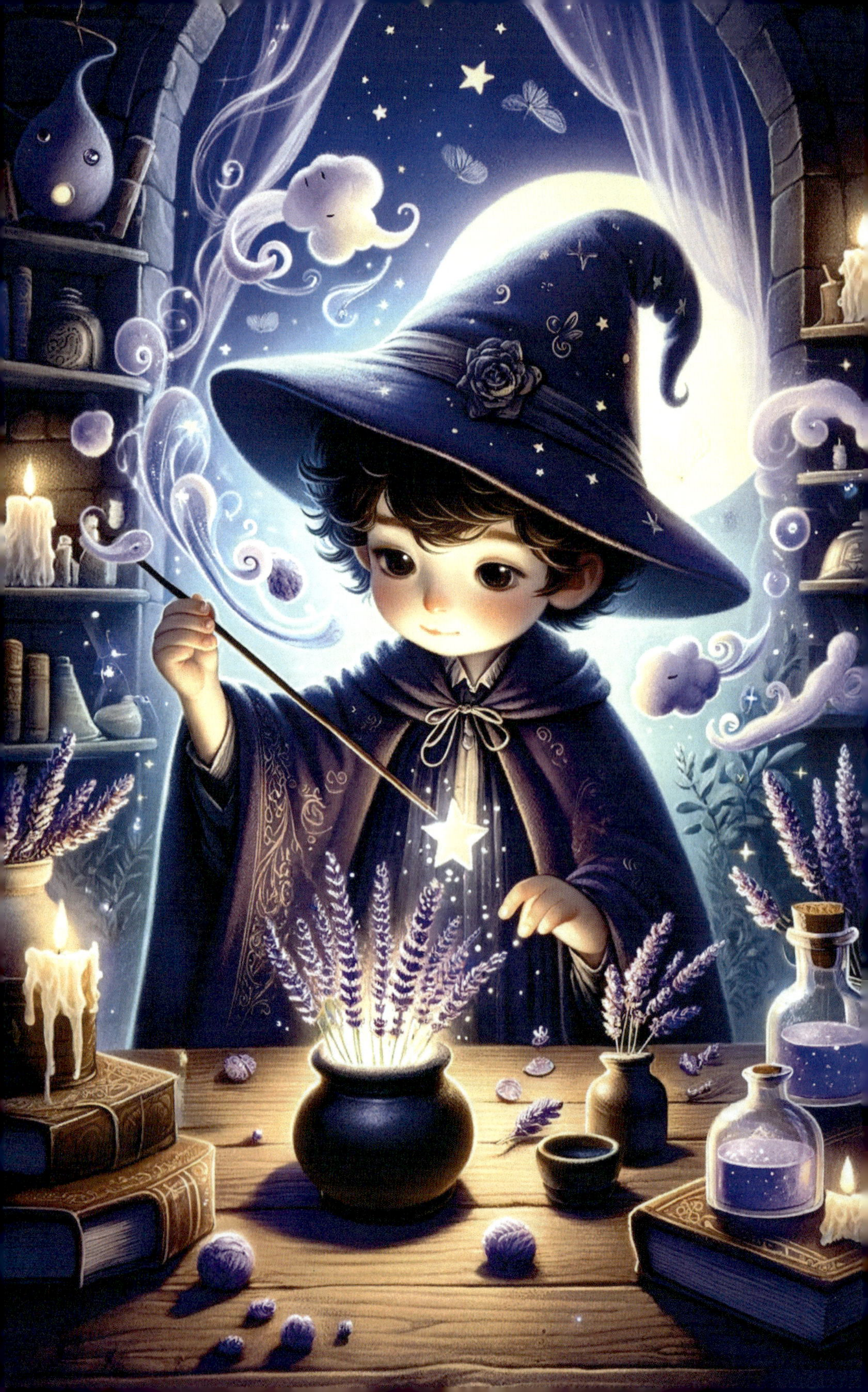

Sweet Dream Spell

Purpose: To encourage sweet and peaceful dreams.

Magical Ingredients:

- A Pillowcase - Your vessel for dreams.
- A Teaspoon of Lavender - For relaxation and calming the mind (can be fresh lavender, dried lavender, or a drop of lavender oil).
- A Small Fabric Star - To guide your dreams to pleasant realms.
- Magic Wand - For directing your peaceful intentions.
- Moonlight Water - Water that has been left to bask in the moonlight for a night.

Directions:
- Prepare Your Space: Choose a quiet time before bed. Place your pillowcase on your bed, ready to be infused with magic.
- Lavender & Star: Sprinkle the lavender into the pillowcase and place the fabric star inside. These are your dream guides.
- Charge with Moonlight Water: With your magic wand, gently sprinkle a few drops of moonlight water over the pillowcase while focusing on peaceful, happy dreams.
- Recite the Chant: Holding your magic wand, gently wave it over your pillowcase and recite the magical chant:

> "Lavender's calm and star so bright,
> In my pillowcase, sleep tonight.
> Dreams be sweet and rest be deep,
> Into dreamland, let me leap."

- Final Touch: Place your pillowcase on your pillow and fluff it gently, letting the magic settle in.
- Believe in Sweet Dreams: As you lay down, close your eyes and imagine being surrounded by soothing lavender and starlight, guiding you into a night of sweet dreams.
- Rest Peacefully: Drift off to sleep, knowing that your Dreamy Sleep Spell will protect your dreams and ensure a restful night.

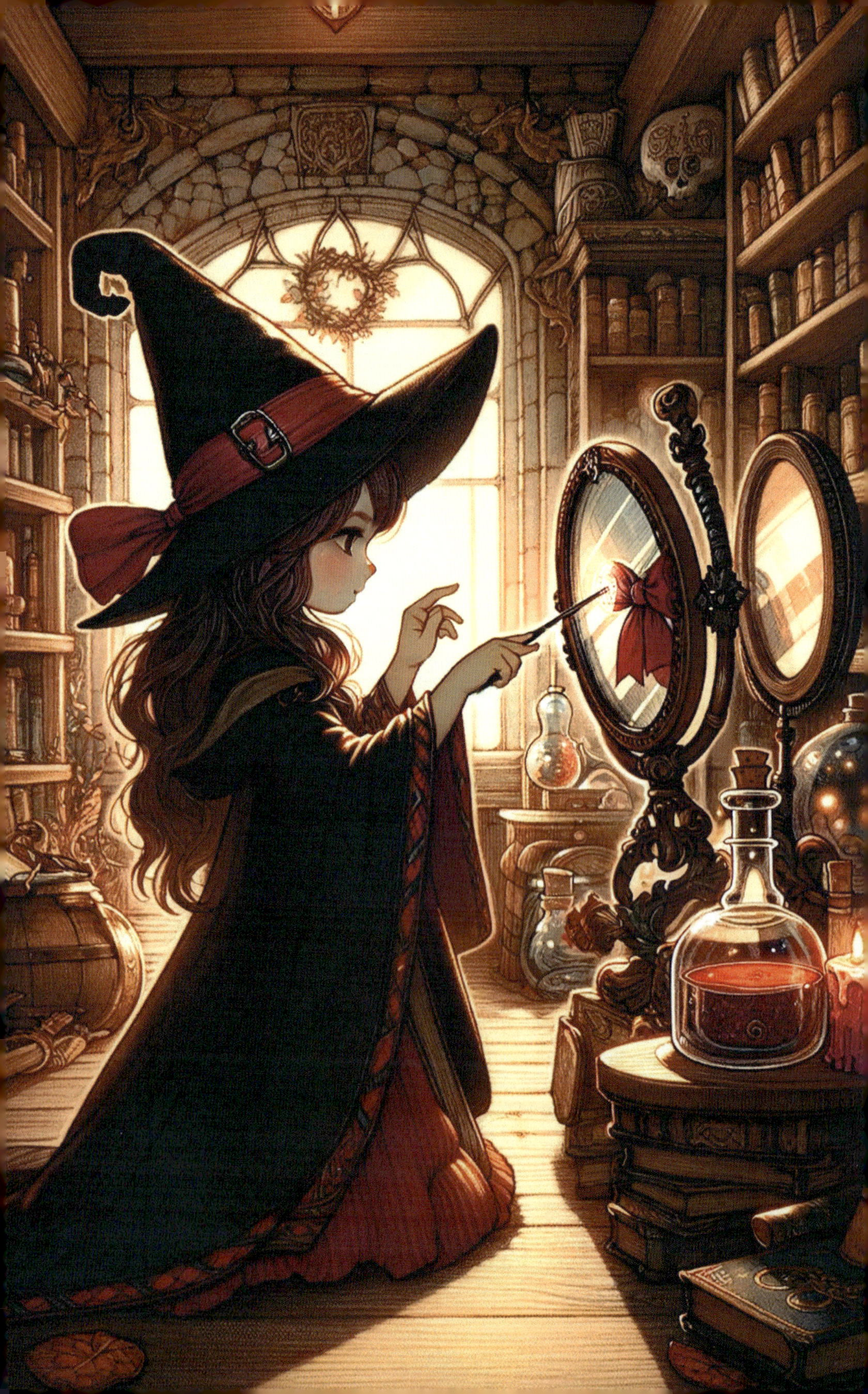

Confidence Charm

Purpose: To enhance self-confidence and inner strength.

Magical Ingredients:

- A Red Ribbon - Symbolizes strength, courage, and confidence.
- A Small Mirror - To reflect your true, confident self.
- A Shiny Coin - Represents wealth in confidence and self-assurance.
- Magic Wand - For focusing and directing your confident energy.
- Sunshine Water - Water that has been left in the sunlight to absorb its bright, positive energy.

Directions:
- Prepare Your Space: Choose a spot where you feel most comfortable and secure. Lay out your magical ingredients with intention.
- Ribbon & Coin: Tie the shiny coin with the red ribbon. This charm is your talisman of confidence.
- Mirror Magic: Hold the small mirror in your hand and look into it. See yourself filled with confidence and strength.
- Charge with Sunshine Water: Use your magic wand to sprinkle sunshine water over the ribbon and coin while focusing on your inner strengths.
- Recite the Chant: Holding your confidence charm, look into the mirror and recite the magical chant:

> "Ribbon red, in confidence wrap,
> Mirror shine, no courage gap.
> Coin that glimmers like the sun,
> Confident, I stand as one."

- Wear the Charm: Tie the ribbon with the coin around your wrist or keep it in your pocket as a constant reminder of your strength and confidence.
- Believe in Yourself: Feel the power of the charm boost your confidence. Remember, true confidence comes from within.

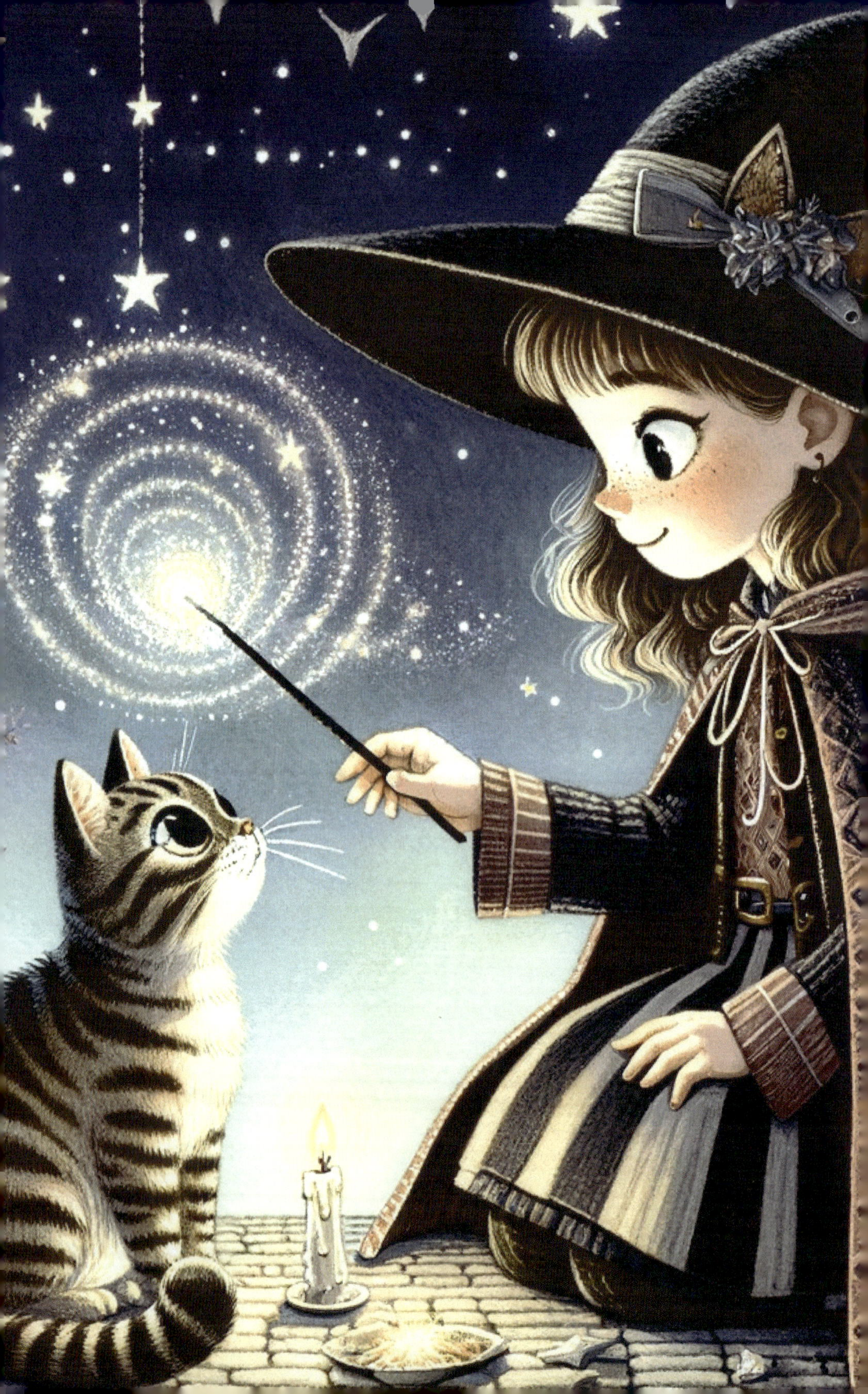

Talk to Animals

Purpose: To enhance empathy and understanding towards animals and to feel a deeper connection with nature.

Magical Ingredients:
- A Feather - Represents the creatures of the sky and the lightness of communication.
- A Small Bowl of Water - Symbolizes the fluidity of understanding and the creatures of the water.
- A Picture or Drawing of a Favorite Animal - Helps to focus your intentions on a specific animal or all animals in general.

Directions:
- Prepare Your Space: Choose a peaceful spot where you can feel close to nature, like near a window or in a garden.
- Feather and Water: Place the feather beside the bowl of water. These elements represent your connection to all animals, from the birds in the sky to the fish in the sea.
- Animal Focus: Place the picture or drawing of your chosen animal next to the bowl.
- Recite the Chant: Gently hold the picture or touch the drawing, and with the feather and bowl of water in sight, recite the magical chant:

> "Feather soft and water clear,
> Call the animals, draw them near.
> With this picture, I reach out,
> Nature's whispers, all about."

- Connect with Nature: Take a moment to quietly observe the nature around you, imagining a gentle exchange of understanding between you and the animals.
- Believe in the Magic: While this spell won't make animals talk like humans, it's a wonderful way to enhance your appreciation and understanding of them. Imagine listening to their needs and living harmoniously alongside them.
- Practice Kindness: Use this spell as a reminder to be kind and respectful to all creatures. The true magic lies in empathy and care for our animal friends.

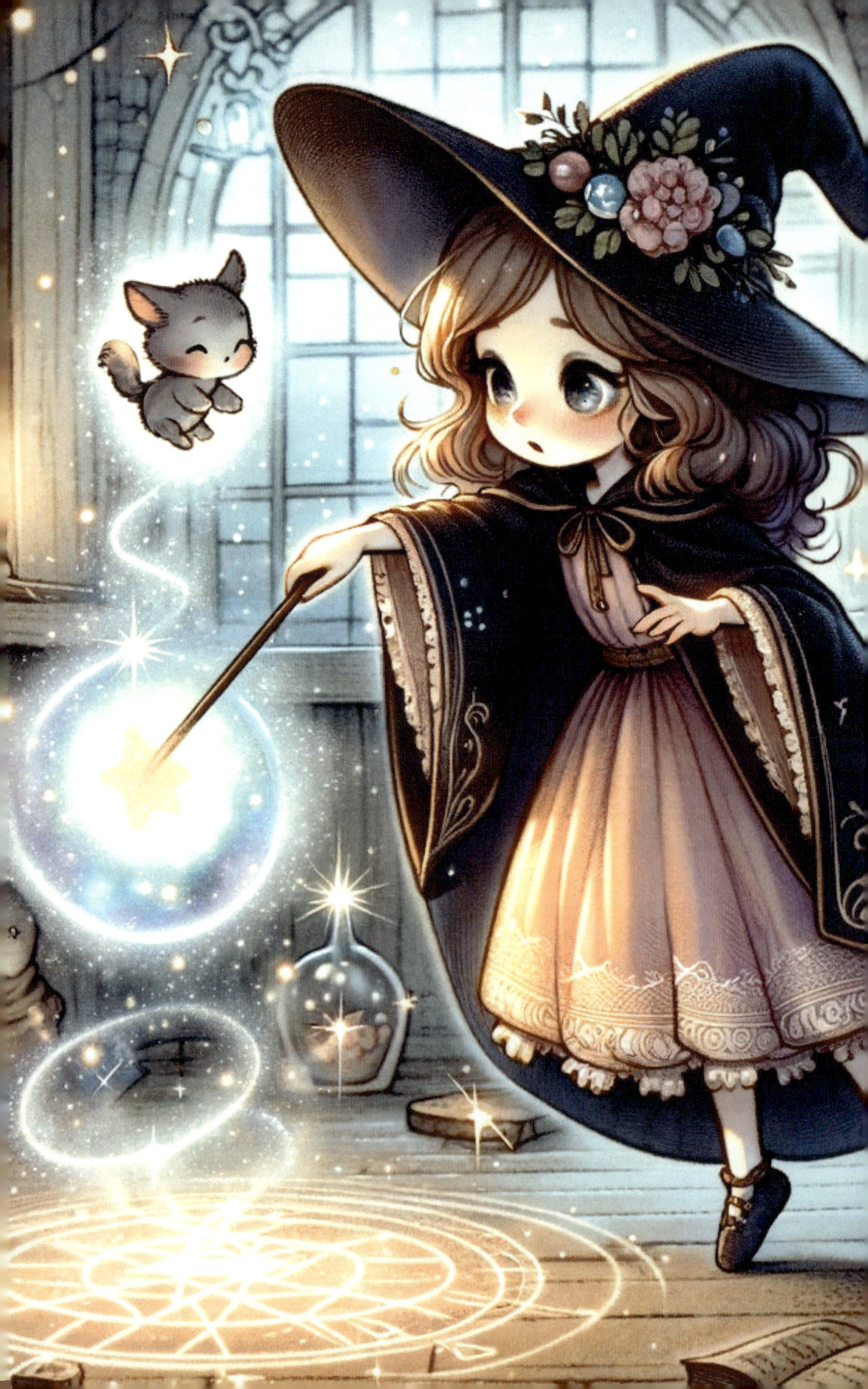

Flying Spell

Purpose: To imagine the exhilarating experience of flying freely through the sky.

Magical Ingredients:
- A Feather - Symbolizes lightness and the ability to glide through the air.
- A Blue Scarf or Piece of Fabric - Represents the sky and freedom of flight.
- A Small Wind Chime or Bell - Mimics the sounds of the wind and the heights of the sky.

Directions:
- Prepare Your Launch Area: Find a safe and open space where you can move around freely. This could be your backyard, a park, or a spacious room.
- Lay Out the Blue Fabric: Spread the blue scarf or fabric on the ground, symbolizing your personal patch of sky.
- Hold the Feather: Grasp the feather in your hand, feeling its lightness and imagining it giving you the ability to fly.
- Ring the Wind Chime or Bell: Gently ring the chime or bell, listening to the sounds and imagining them as the wind whooshing past you as you soar.
- Recite the Chant: Stand on the edge of your blue fabric 'sky', close your eyes, raise your arms like wings, and recite the magical chant:

> "Feather light and sky so blue,
> Lift me up, into the view.
> Wind's sweet song, carry me high,
> Soaring, gliding through the sky."

- Visualize Flying: With your arms still raised, imagine yourself lifting off the ground, flying over landscapes, feeling the freedom and exhilaration of flight.
- Enjoy the Imagined Flight: Run around your 'sky', mimicking the movements of flying, feeling the joy and freedom.
- Gently Land: When you're ready to 'land', slow down, lower your arms, and step off the blue fabric, feeling the gentle return to earth.

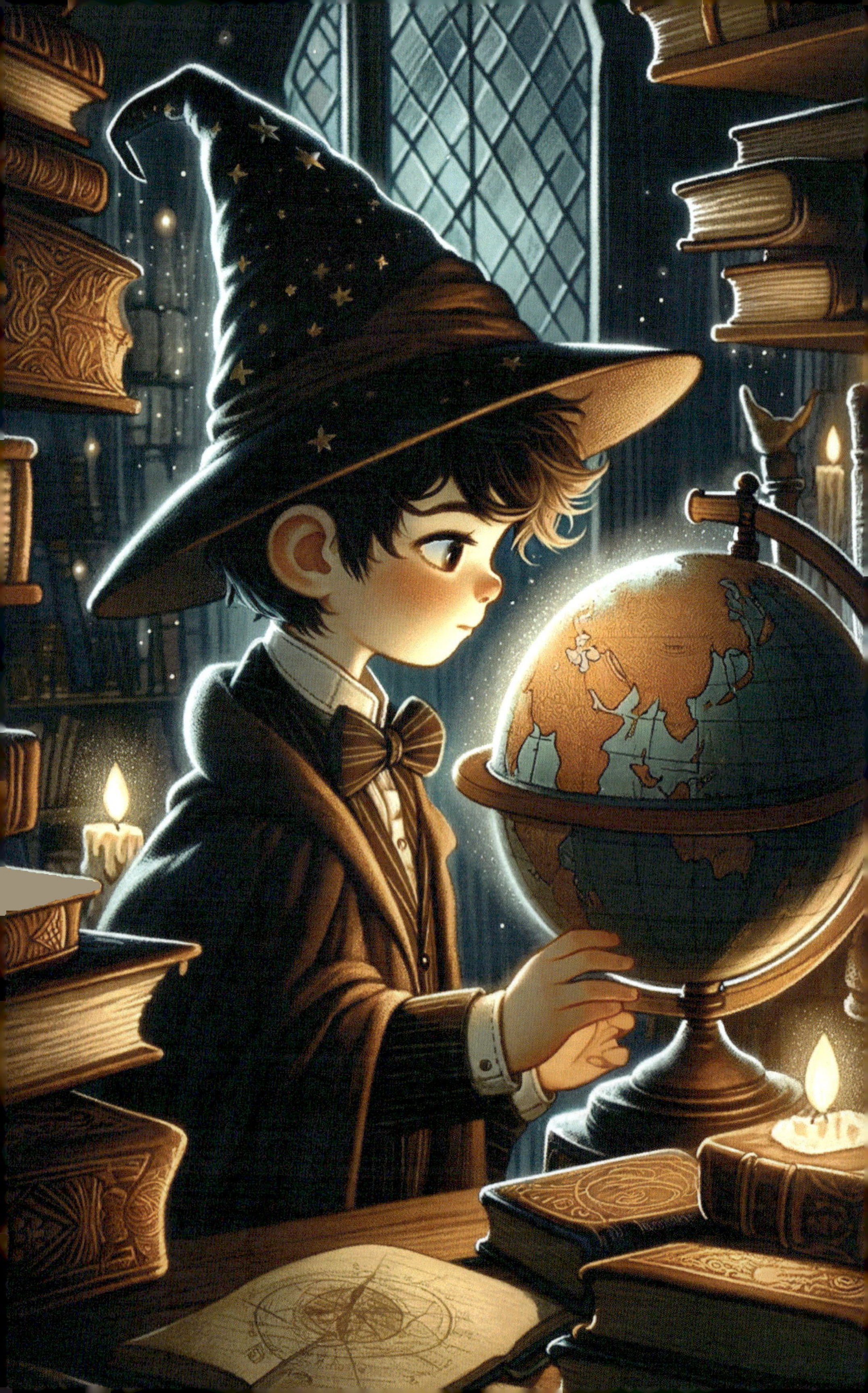

Study Spell

Purpose: To enhance focus, understanding, and enjoyment in learning.

Magical Ingredients:
- A Bookmark or Small Piece of Paper - To symbolize the journey through knowledge.
- A Pencil or Pen - Represents the tool of learning and comprehension.
- A Small Globe or Map - Symbolizes the vast world of knowledge to be explored.
- Three Peppermint Leaves - For clarity of mind and concentration (can be fresh or dried).

Directions:
- Prepare Your Space: Find a peaceful spot where you usually study or do homework. Lay out your magical ingredients before you.
- Create the Scholar's Circle: Place the bookmark or piece of paper in front of you, lay the pencil or pen across it, and set the small globe or map beside them. Arrange the peppermint leaves around these items in a triangle.
- Recite the Chant: Focus on the items in your Scholar's Circle, and with a desire to learn, recite the magical chant:

> "Bookmark guide and pencil true,
> World of knowledge, I pursue.
> Peppermint clear, my mind awake,
> Ease of learning, I shall take."

- Empower Your Tools: Pick up the pencil or pen and wave it gently over the circle, imagining it absorbing the magic of focus and understanding.
- Conclude with Belief: Place the bookmark in a book you're currently studying, carry the pencil with you to school, and believe in your enhanced ability to learn and understand.
- Use the Magic: Approach your studies with this newfound confidence and focus, reminding yourself of the spell whenever you face a challenging topic.

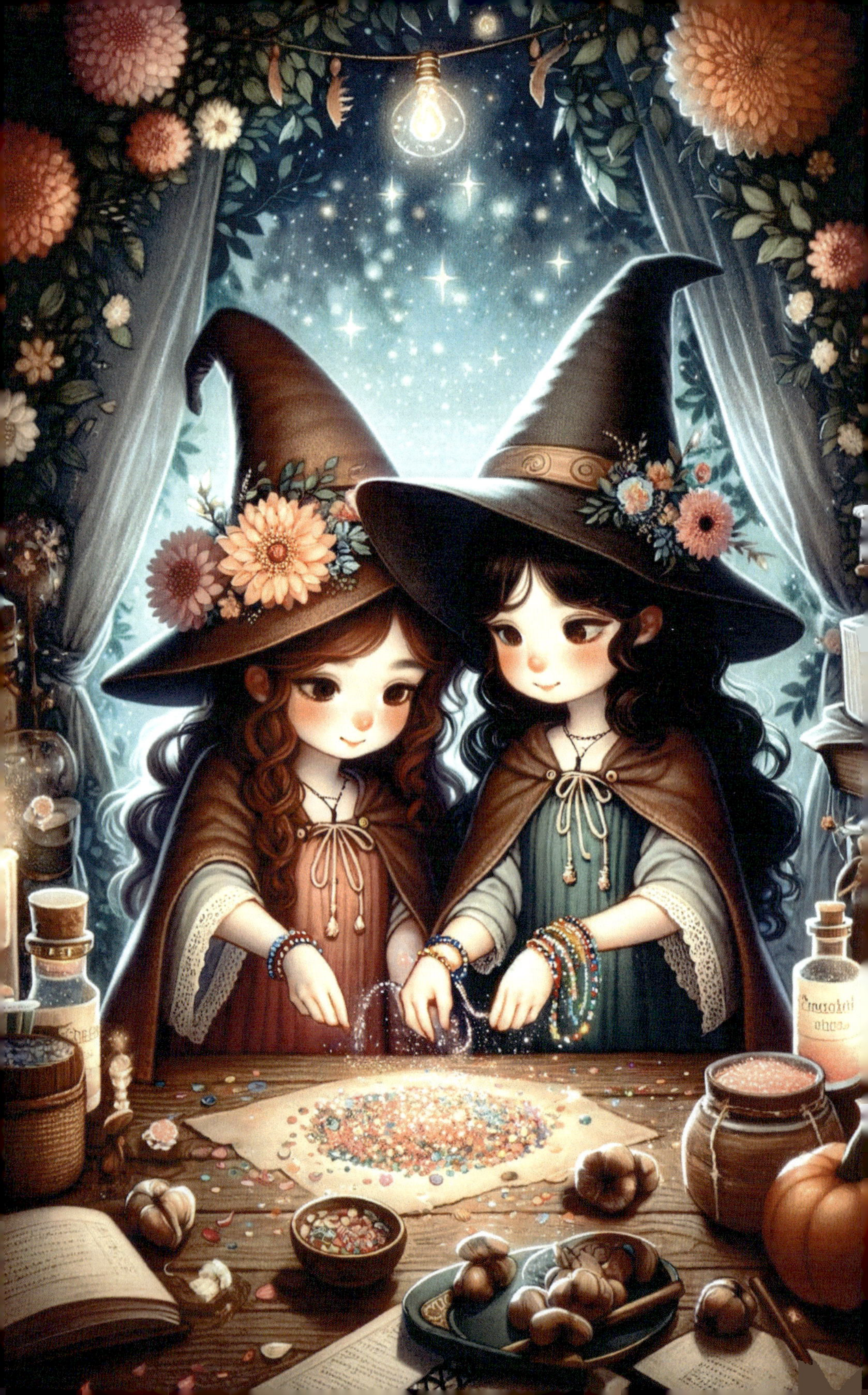

Friendship Blossom Spell

Purpose: To nurture and celebrate existing friendships and to open the heart to new ones.

Magical Ingredients:
- Colorful Flower Petals - Each petal represents a unique aspect of friendship.
- A Friendship Bracelet or a Piece of String - Symbolizes the bond between friends.
- A Small Note - Write the name of a friend or friends you cherish, or a wish for a new friendship.

Directions:
- Prepare Your Space: Find a cozy and comfortable spot where you feel happy and at peace. This spell is best done thinking about happy memories with friends.
- Petals and Bracelet/String: Place the flower petals in your pouch or container. If you have a friendship bracelet, place it inside; if not, tie the string into a circle and place it with the petals.
- Write the Note: On your small note, write down the name(s) of your friend(s) or your wish for a new friend. Fold the note and place it in the pouch.
- Recite the Chant: Hold the pouch in your hands, close your eyes, and recite the magical chant with heartfelt sincerity:

>"Petals bright and bracelet tied,
>Friendship grows, side by side.
>Names we whisper, hearts we share,
>Magic blooms in the air."

- Seal the Spell: Tie the pouch closed, sealing the magic of friendship inside.
- Believe in Friendship: Carry the pouch with you or place it somewhere special. Believe in the power of friendship and the bonds you've celebrated and wished for.
- Share the Joy: Remember, the best way to grow a friendship is to share kindness, laughter, and support. Use this spell as a reminder of that magic.

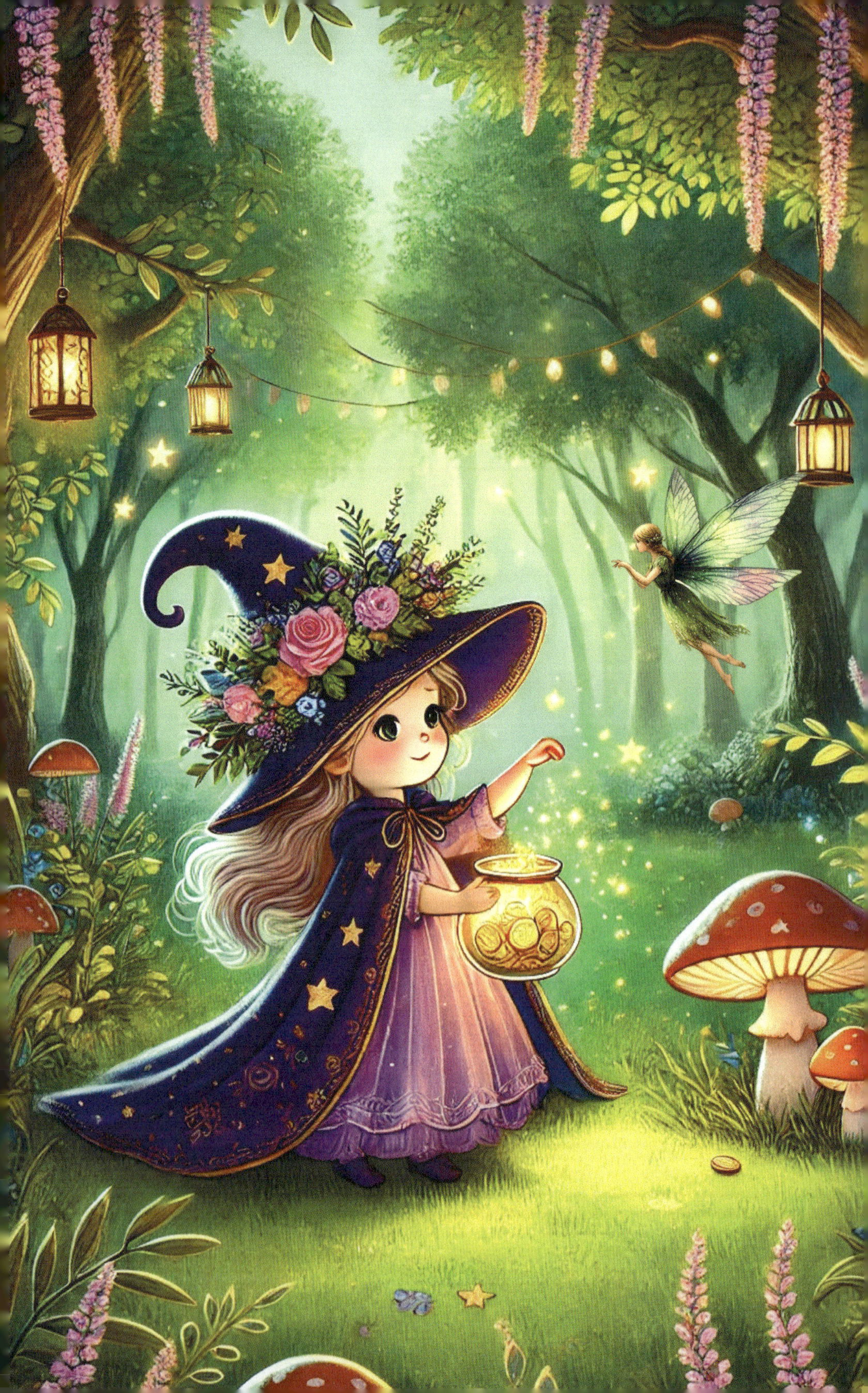

Fairy Summoning Spell

Purpose: To invite the mystical presence of fairies into your garden or room, in the spirit of enchantment and whimsy.

Magical Ingredients:
- Flower Petals - Various colors to attract the fairies with beauty.
- A Small Bell - Its gentle ring is said to be irresistible to fairies.
- A Shiny Coin or Sequin - To catch the light and draw fairies near.
- A Spoonful of Honey - To offer sweetness and hospitality to the fairies.

Directions:
- Prepare Your Space: Choose a peaceful spot where you feel a connection to nature. This could be in your garden, near a plant in your home, or by a window.
- Lay Out the Petals: Arrange the flower petals in a circle, creating a beautiful and inviting space for the fairies.
- Ring the Bell: Gently ring the small bell three times to send out an invitation to the fairies.
- Place the Coin and Honey: Set the shiny coin or sequin in the center of the petal circle as a sparkling beacon. Next to it, place the spoonful of honey as a sweet gift.
- Recite the Chant: Stand or sit quietly beside your fairy circle, and with a whisper of excitement, recite the magical chant:

>"Petals bright and bell so clear,
>Fairies near, please come here.
>Shine and honey, gifts we lay,
>Join us in the light of day."

- Wait and Watch: Sit quietly and watch for signs of the fairies. You might not see them, but perhaps you'll feel their presence or notice small movements in nature.
- Express Gratitude: Whether you sense the fairies or not, thank them for their magic and the joy they bring to the world.

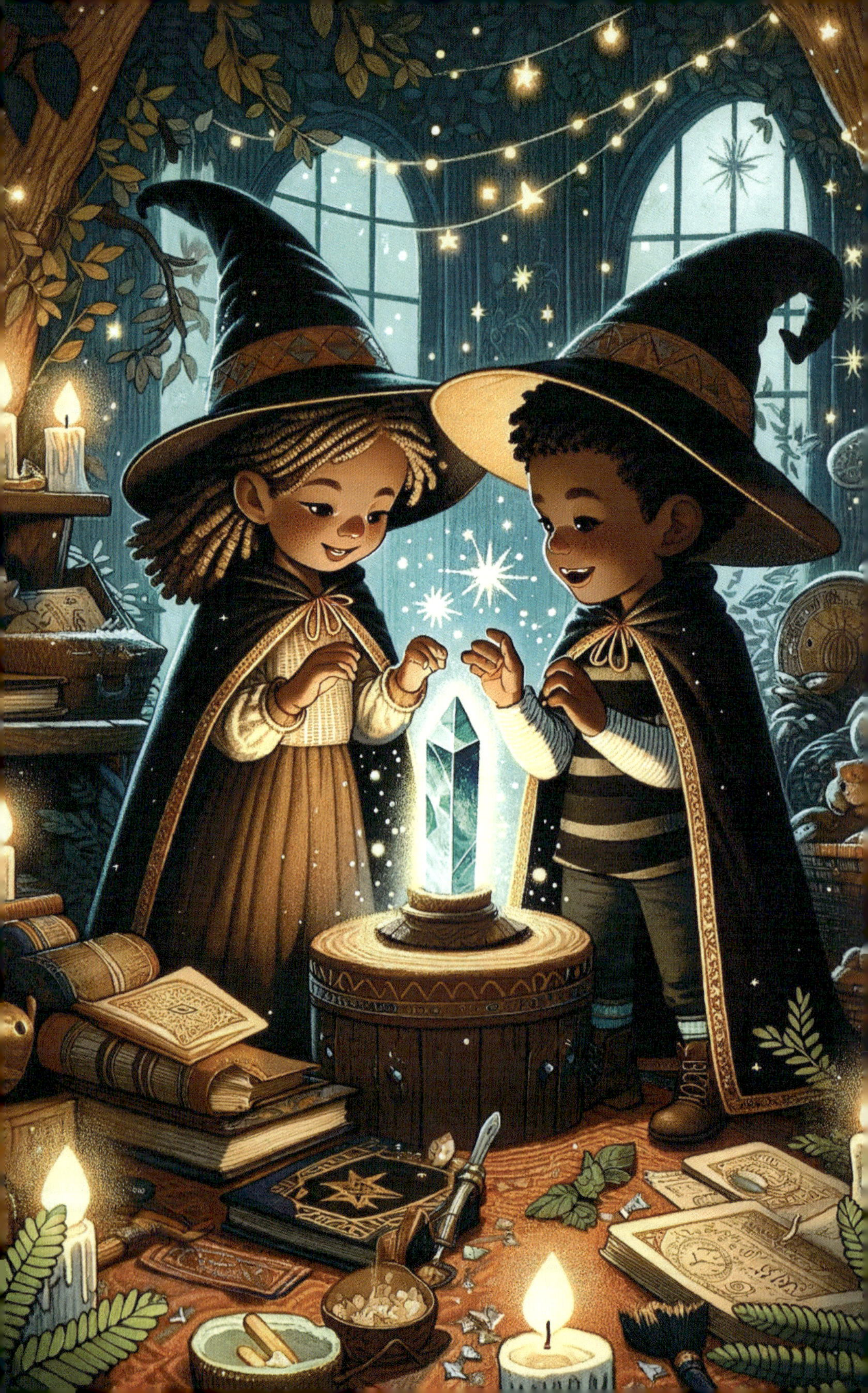

Finder's Light

Purpose: To aid in recalling and locating a lost item.

Magical Ingredients:
- A Candle (LED or real) or a Small Lamp - Represents the light of clarity and discovery.
- A Picture or Representation of the Lost Item - If you don't have a picture, a small drawing or written description will do.
- A Piece of String or Ribbon - Symbolizes the connection between you and the lost item.
- A Small Bell - Its sound is believed to clear confusion and bring insight.

Directions:
- Prepare Your Space: Choose a quiet area where you can concentrate. Lay out your magical ingredients.
- Illuminate the Candle or Lamp: Light the candle (or turn on the lamp), letting its light symbolize clarity and insight.
- Connect with the Item: Place the picture or representation of the lost item in front of the light. Tie the string or ribbon around it, connecting it to the candle or lamp, representing your connection to the item.
- Ring the Bell: Gently ring the bell to clear the air and your mind, creating a space of focus and clarity.
- Recite the Chant: Focus on the representation of the lost item, and with a clear mind, recite the magical chant:

> "Light that shines and bell that rings,
> Guide me to my missing things.
> String that binds, bring to light,
> What is lost, now in sight."

- Visualize Finding the Item: Close your eyes and visualize finding the lost item. Imagine where it might be, retracing your steps in your mind.
- Trust and Act: Extinguish the candle (or turn off the lamp) and untie the string, believing that you will find your lost item. Start looking again, this time with a clear and focused mind.

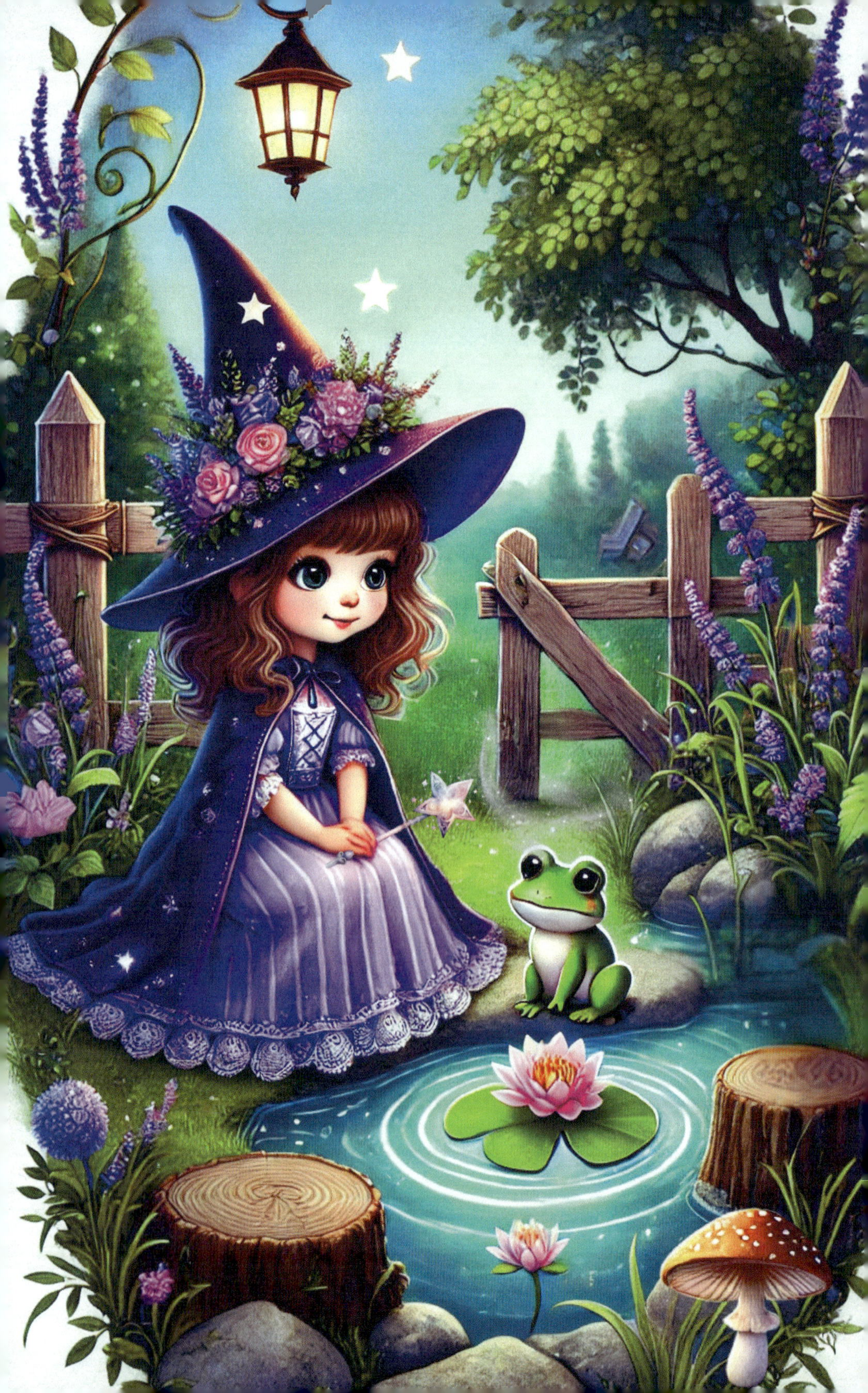

Frog Transformation

Purpose: To playfully imagine turning someone into a frog, in the spirit of fun and fantasy.

Magical Ingredients:
- A Small Toy Frog - Represents the transformation.
- Green Construction Paper - Symbolizes the color and essence of a frog.
- A Small Cup of Water - For the frog's natural habitat.
- A Picture or Drawing of the Person - To focus the spell (use a drawing or a toy figure for a more imaginative and respectful approach).

Directions:
- Prepare Your Space: Find a comfortable area where laughter and play are welcome. Lay out your magical ingredients.
- Create the Frog Circle: Place the green construction paper on the ground and set the toy frog in the center. Pour the cup of water around the frog, not too close, creating a small 'pond'.
- Place the Picture or Drawing: Set the picture or drawing of the person (or toy figure) next to the frog.
- Recite the Chant: With a smile and a giggle, recite the magical chant:

    "With a ribbit and a hop, transformation won't stop,
    Turn now, from toe to top, into a frog with a leap and a plop!"

- Enact the Transformation: Tap the picture or drawing (or toy figure) with a finger, playfully imagining it turning into the toy frog.
- Reverse the Spell: After enjoying the moment, reverse the spell with a simple wave over the toy frog and picture, saying, "Back you go, to your true form, as this spell was just to inform!"

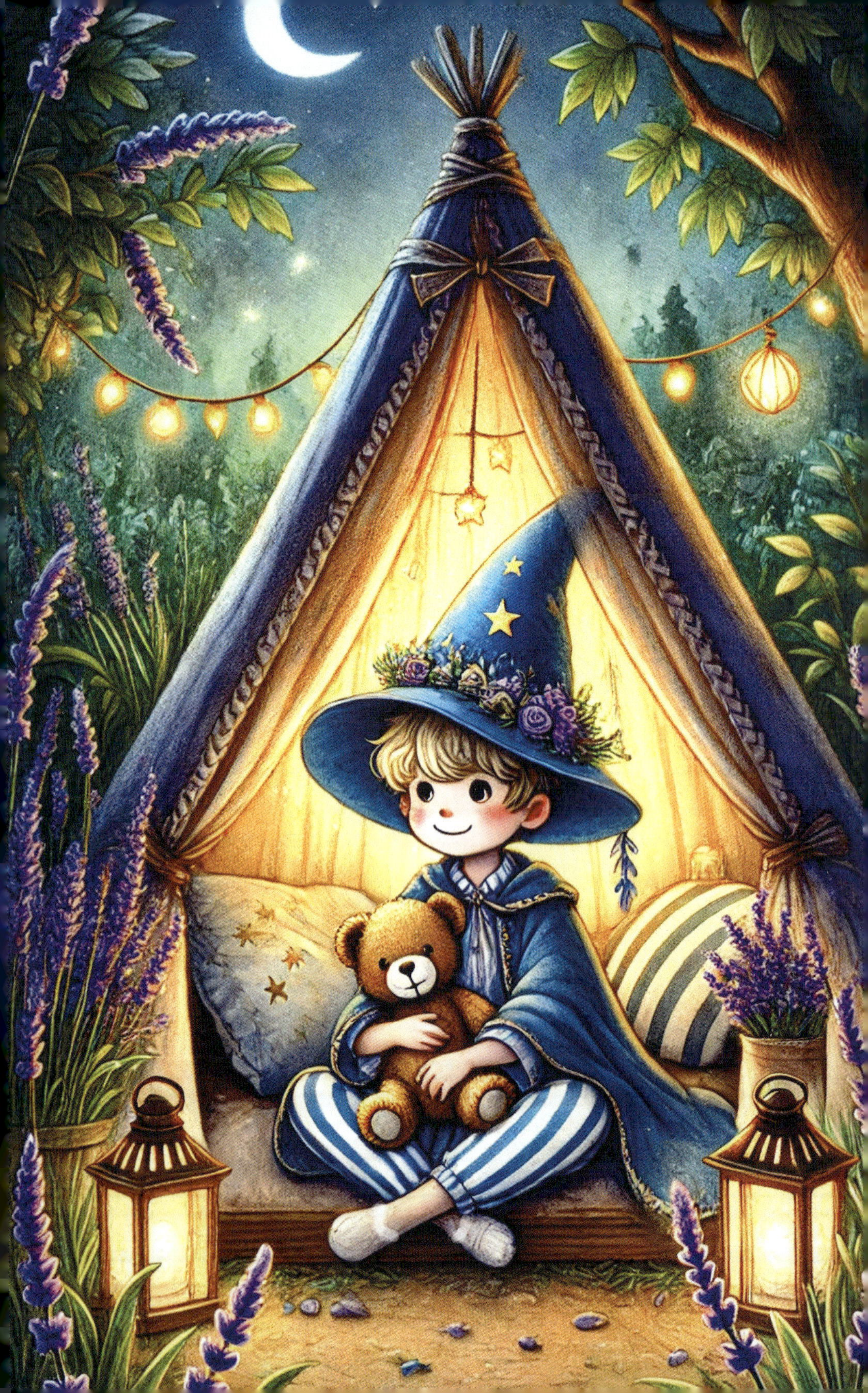

Safe Space Spell

Purpose: To create an invisible sanctuary of calm and safety, providing comfort during moments of anxiety or stress.

Magical Ingredients:
- A Small Comforting Object - This could be a smooth stone, a soft piece of fabric, or a small toy that brings you comfort.
- A Lavender Sachet or a Few Drops of Lavender Oil - Known for its calming properties.
- A Piece of Blue or Green Fabric - Representing tranquility and peace.
- A Quiet, Comforting Chant or Song - Something that soothes you, even hummed softly.

Directions:
- Prepare Your Space: Find a quiet spot where you can sit or lie down comfortably. Lay the piece of fabric on your lap or beside you.
- Place Your Comfort Object: Hold your comforting object in your hands, feeling its texture and presence.
- Introduce Lavender: If using a sachet, place it beside you; if using oil, gently dab a small amount on your wrists or the fabric.
- Recite the Chant or Hum Your Song: Softly chant or hum your chosen soothing sounds. As you do, imagine a bubble of calm light surrounding you, creating a safe space.
- Visualize the Sanctuary: Close your eyes and imagine your sanctuary. Visualize it filled with calming colors, gentle light, and a sense of peace.
- Breathe Deeply: Take slow, deep breaths, inhaling the calming scent of lavender, and exhaling any tension or worry.
- Affirm Your Safety: Whisper to yourself, "I am safe, I am calm, I am at peace."

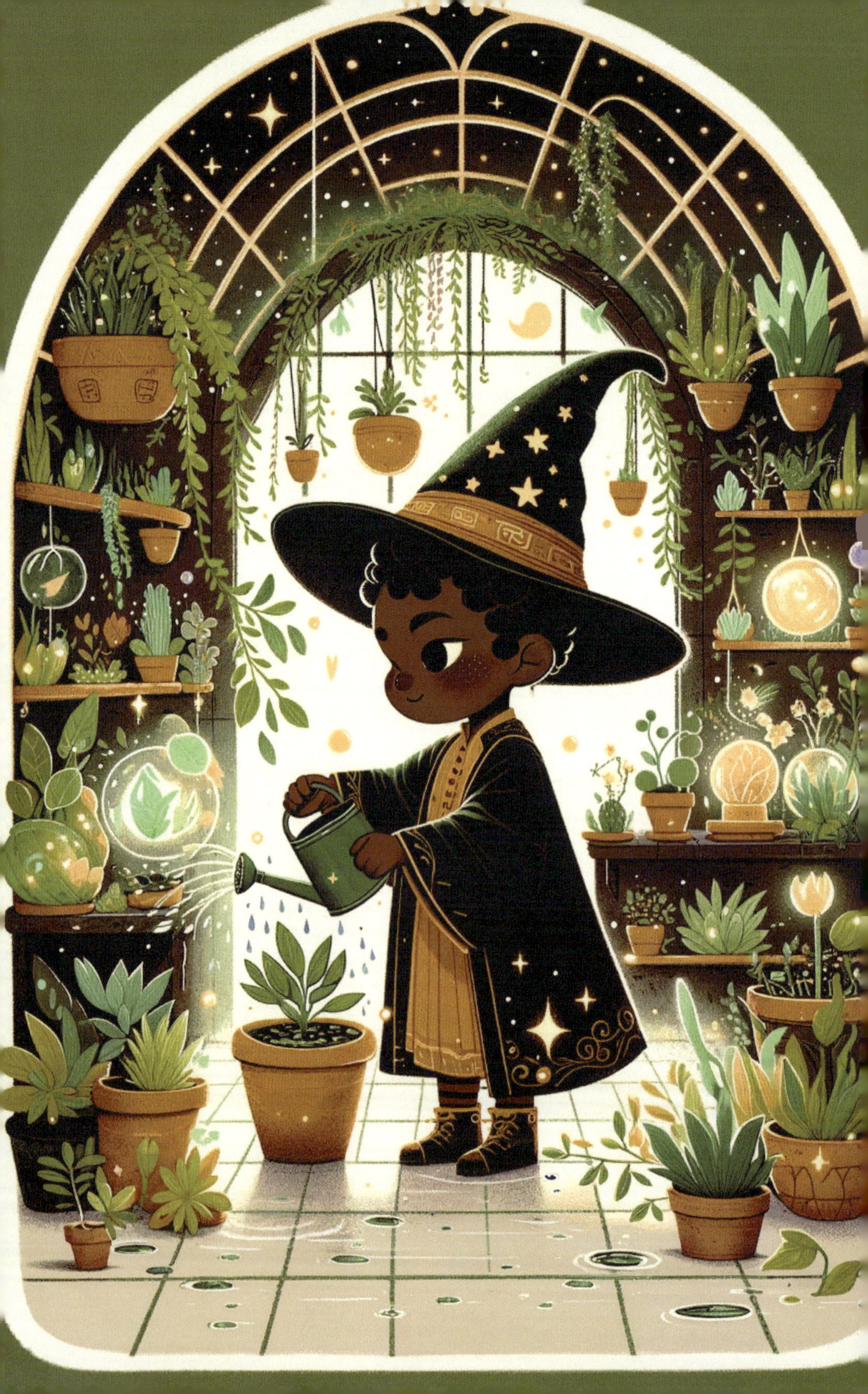

Green Fingers Charm

Purpose: To encourage the growth and health of a plant through positive intentions and care.

Magical Ingredients:
- A Healthy Plant in Need of Growth - This can be any plant you're currently nurturing.
- A Small Watering Can or Cup of Water - Represents the life-giving resource for all plants.
- A Stone or Crystal - Such as a green aventurine or clear quartz, believed to promote growth and vitality.
- A Spoonful of Nutritious Soil or Compost - Symbolizes the richness and support of the earth.

Directions:
- Prepare Your Space: Approach your plant with a gentle and caring mindset. Place the stone or crystal near the base of the plant.
- Enrich the Soil: Sprinkle the spoonful of nutritious soil or compost around the base of the plant, imagining it providing the necessary nutrients for growth.
- Water the Plant: Gently water the plant with your watering can or cup of water, visualizing the water as a source of vitality and life.
- Recite the Chant: As you care for your plant, recite the magical chant:

> "Water and stone, earth's rich boon,
> Grant this plant the strength to bloom.
> Roots grow deep, leaves reach high,
> Thrive and flourish, towards the sky."

- Visualize the Growth: Close your eyes and imagine your plant growing strong, healthy, and vibrant. Picture its roots deepening and its leaves expanding.
- Conclude with Gratitude: Finish the ritual by expressing your gratitude to the plant for its beauty and presence in your life.

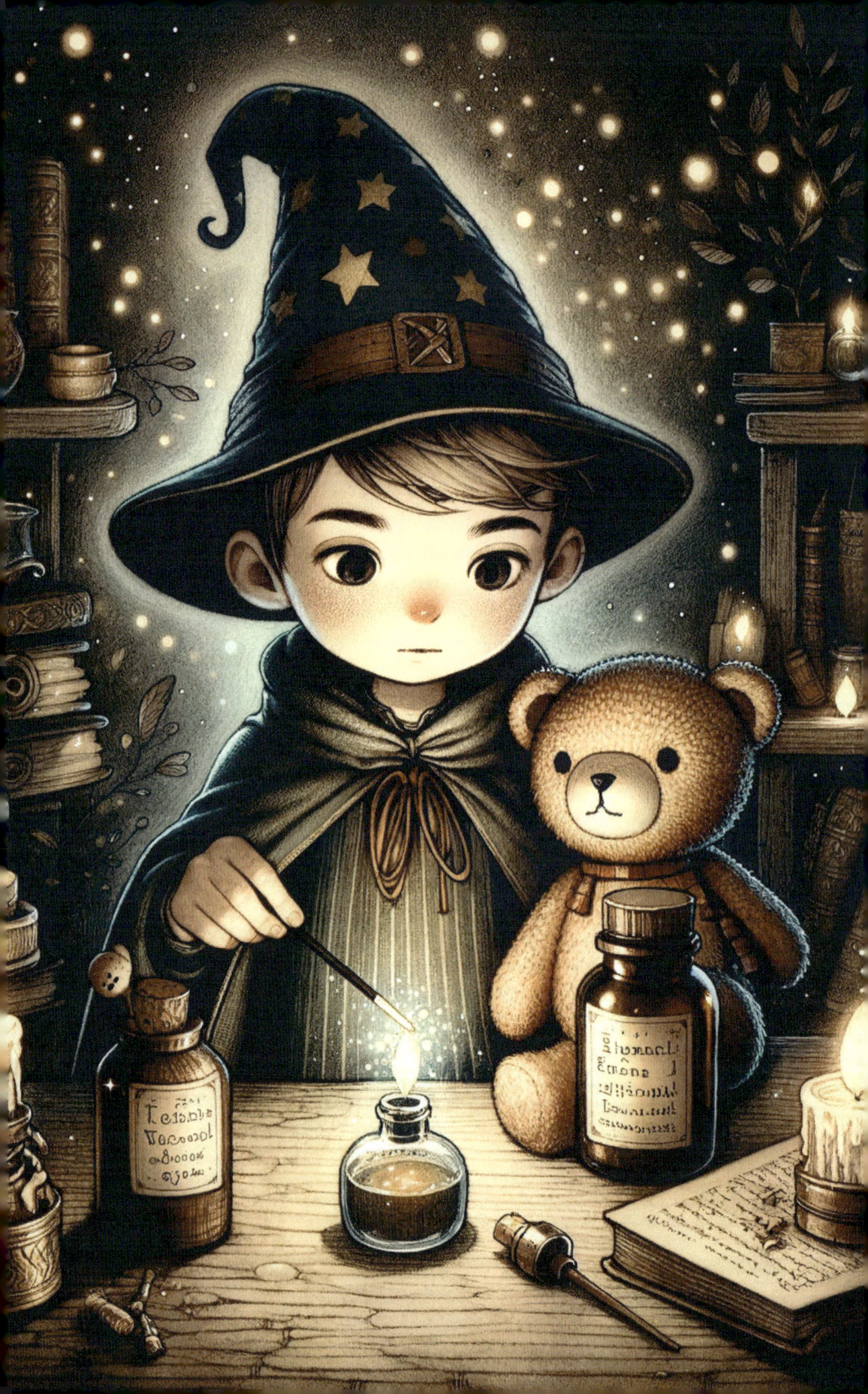

Monster Banishing Spell

Purpose: To provide comfort and a sense of security by playfully banishing any imaginary monsters lurking under the bed.

Magical Ingredients:
- A Small Flashlight or Nightlight - To shine light into dark places and dispel shadows.
- A Stuffed Animal or Protective Toy - As a guardian to watch over you while you sleep.
- A Sprinkle of Lavender or a Lavender Sachet - For its calming and soothing properties.
- A Protective Chant - Words to empower and reassure.

Directions:
- Prepare Your Space: As bedtime approaches, gather your magical ingredients and approach your bed with confidence.
- Illuminate the Darkness: Turn on the flashlight or nightlight and briefly shine it under the bed, dispelling shadows and bringing light to dark corners.
- Place the Guardian: Put the stuffed animal or protective toy at the foot of your bed, facing under it, to stand guard through the night.
- Lavender for Calmness: Place the lavender or sachet nearby, allowing its soothing scent to fill the air.
- Recite the Chant: With a strong and brave voice, recite the magical chant:

> "Monsters lurking, now be gone,
> Leave my room, don't linger on.
> Guardians watch, light shines through,
> In this space, only peace and calm ensue."

- Believe in Safety: Feel the room become a safe and monster-free zone. Trust in the protection of your guardian and the light.
- Rest Peacefully: Climb into bed, feeling safe and secure. Let the calmness of the lavender and the warmth of your bed embrace you into a peaceful sleep.

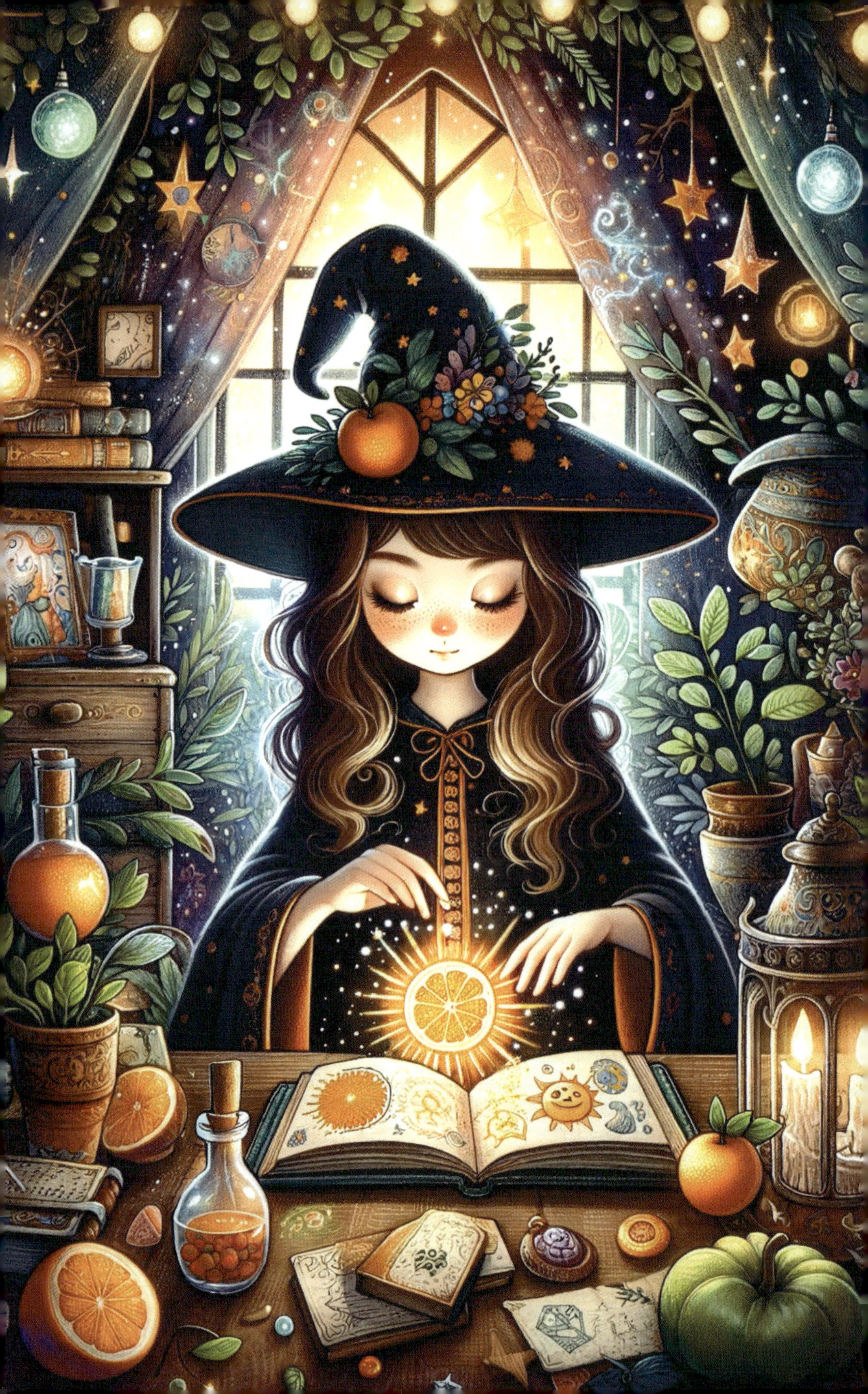

Energy Spell

Purpose: To reinvigorate your energy and dispel feelings of tiredness.

Magical Ingredients:
- A Brightly Colored Fruit - Such as an orange or apple, for natural energy and vitality.
- A Glass of Water - Symbolizing refreshment and rejuvenation.
- A Small Sprig of Mint - Known for its invigorating properties.
- A Sun Symbol - This could be a drawing of the sun or a small item that represents sunlight and energy to you.

Directions:
- Prepare Your Space: Find a spot where you can move freely. Place the sun symbol in a visible spot.
- Place the Fruit and Water: Set the brightly colored fruit and glass of water near the sun symbol.
- Add the Mint: Place the sprig of mint in the glass of water or beside it.
- Recite the Chant: Stand tall and take a deep breath. With a feeling of awakening, recite the magical chant:

> "Sun that shines and fruit that gives,
> Mint that awakens, in me it lives.
> Water clear, energy spark,
> Banish tiredness, light in the dark."

- Eat and Drink: Slowly eat the piece of fruit, savoring its taste and imagining its natural energy filling you. Sip the water infused with mint.
- Movement Magic: Do a quick stretch or a playful dance, imagining the sun's energy filling you with every move.
- Feel Revived: Take a moment to feel the energy flowing through you, embracing a renewed sense of vitality.

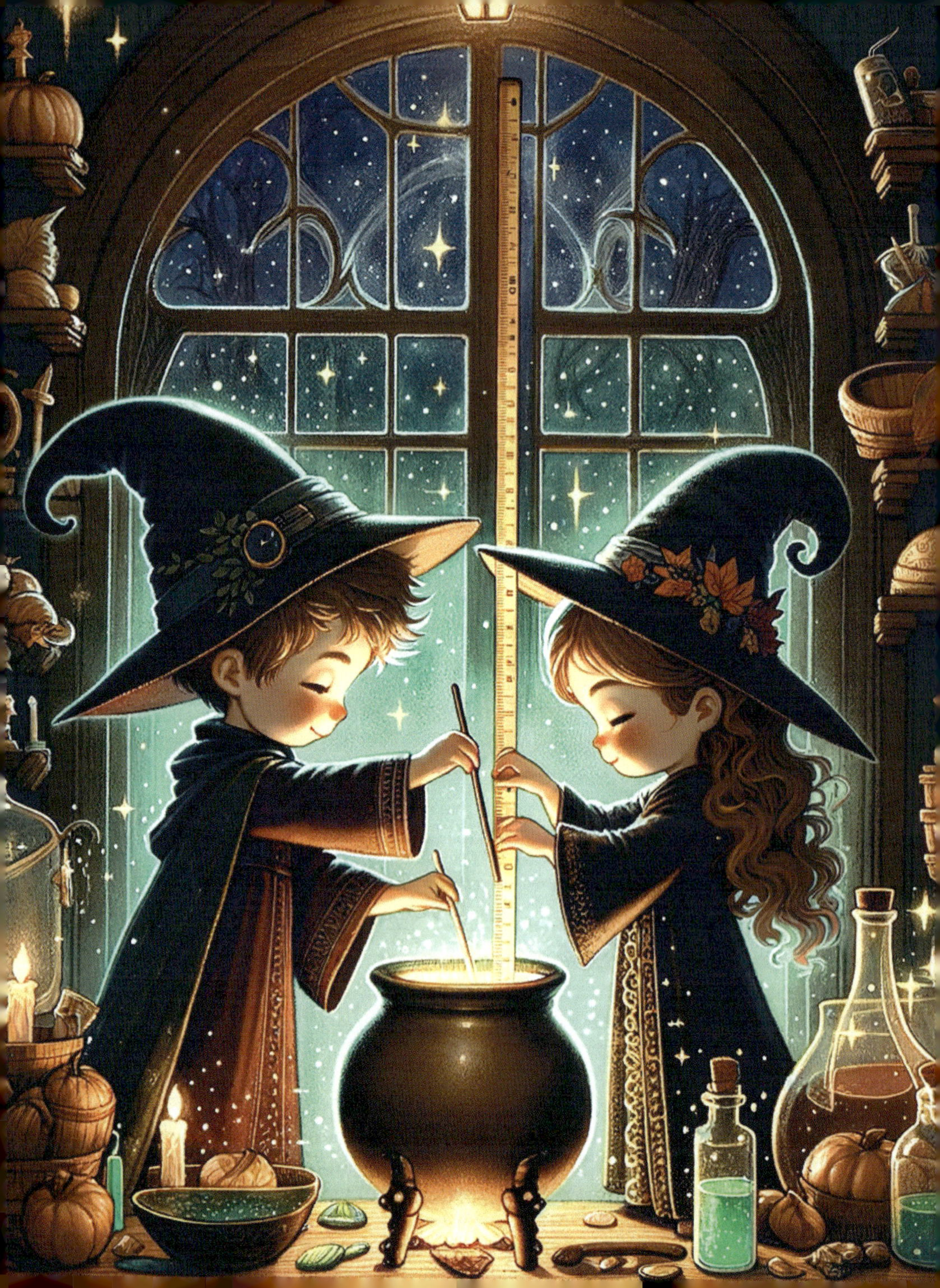

Make me Taller Charm

Purpose: To playfully imagine growing taller, embracing growth and self-confidence.

Magical Ingredients:
- A Growing Plant or Beanstalk - Represents steady and natural growth.
- A Ruler or Measuring Tape - Symbolizes the measurement of growth.
- A Small Bag of Fertile Soil - Signifies the foundation and support for growth.
- A Sun Symbol - Can be a drawing or object; represents the energy and vitality from the sun aiding in growth.

Directions:
- Prepare Your Space: Stand beside the growing plant or beanstalk in an open area where you can stretch comfortably. Lay out the other magical ingredients.
- Place the Soil: Set the bag of fertile soil near your feet, symbolizing a strong and nurturing foundation.
- Hold the Ruler/Measuring Tape: Grasp the ruler or measuring tape, ready to envision your growth.
- Position the Sun Symbol: Place the sun symbol nearby to represent the energy and vitality contributing to your growth.
- Recite the Chant: Stand tall, feet firmly on the ground, and recite the magical chant:

  "Soil below and sun above,
  Aid my growth with light and love.
  Like this plant, I aim to be,
  Growing tall, strong, and free."

- Visualize Growing Taller: Close your eyes and imagine yourself growing taller, like the plant beside you. Feel the strength and vitality in your body.
- Measure for Fun: After the chant, use the ruler or measuring tape to 'measure' your height, playfully noting any 'magical growth'.
- Embrace Your Growth: Acknowledge your current height and growth, remembering that everyone grows at their own pace.

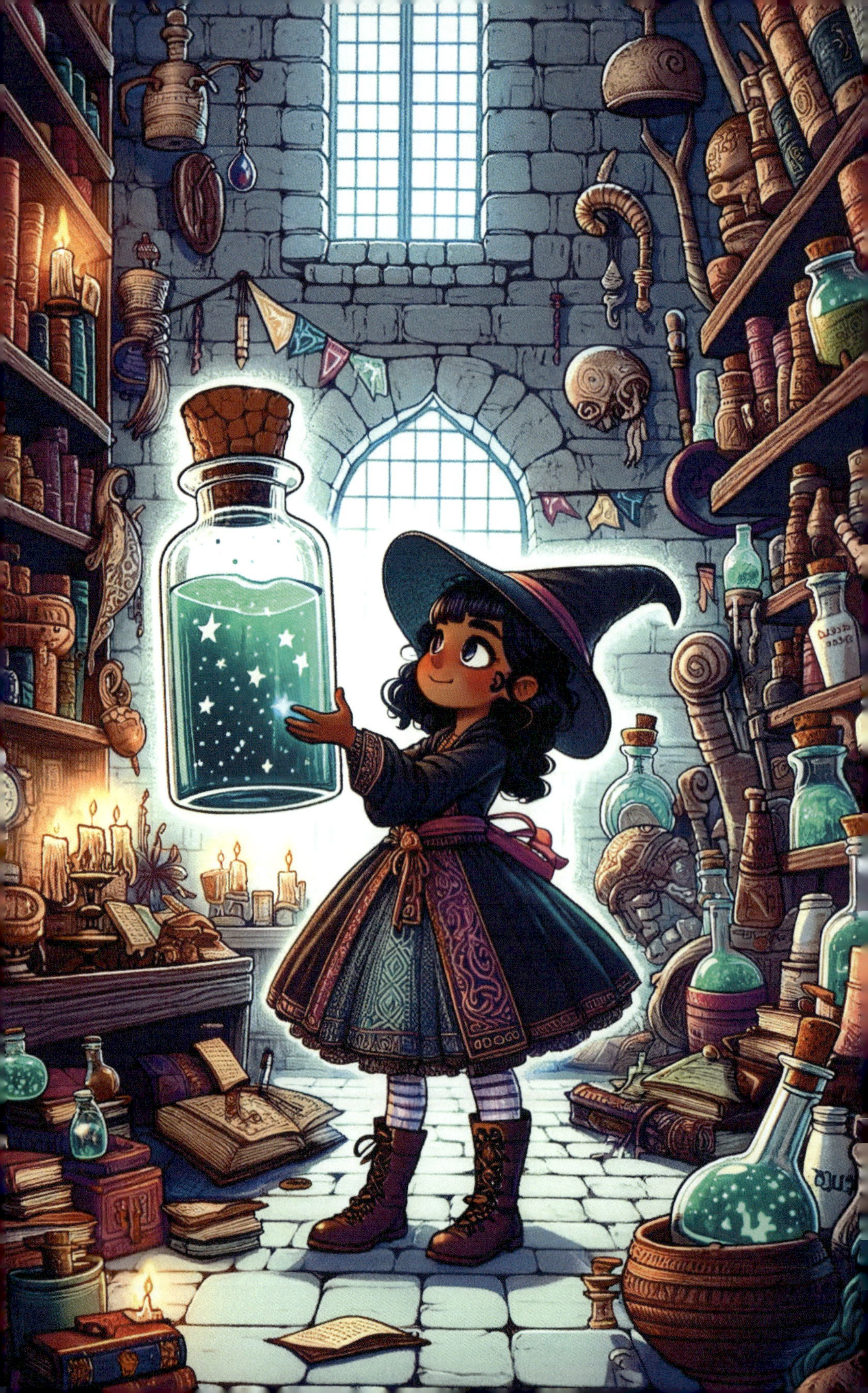

Make Me Tiny Charm

Purpose: To playfully imagine shrinking down to a tiny size and exploring the world from a new viewpoint.

Magical Ingredients:
- A Small Toy or Miniature Object - To represent the shrunken size.
- A Magnifying Glass - Symbolizes seeing the world in a new, enlarged way.
- A Sprig of Thyme - Often associated with smallness and fine detail.
- A Circle of String - Represents the boundary of the shrinking charm.

Directions:
- Prepare Your Space: Find a comfortable area where you can move around safely. Place the miniature object in the center of your space.
- Create the Boundary: Lay the circle of string around the miniature object, creating the area of the shrinking charm.
- Position the Magnifying Glass: Hold the magnifying glass over the miniature object, imagining it as your new, smaller size.
- Place the Thyme: Set the sprig of thyme within the string circle, to add the essence of smallness to your charm.
- Recite the Chant:

> "Tiny as thyme, small and fine,
> Shrink me down, this charm of mine.
> Through the glass, a world anew,
> Miniature sights, a different view."

- Imagine the Transformation: Close your eyes and imagine yourself shrinking down to the size of the toy or object, exploring the world from this new perspective.
- Playful Exploration: Open your eyes and use the magnifying glass to explore your surroundings, pretending to see everything as if you are very small.
- Return to Size: When you're ready to 'grow back', step outside the string circle and stretch up tall, imagining yourself returning to your normal size.

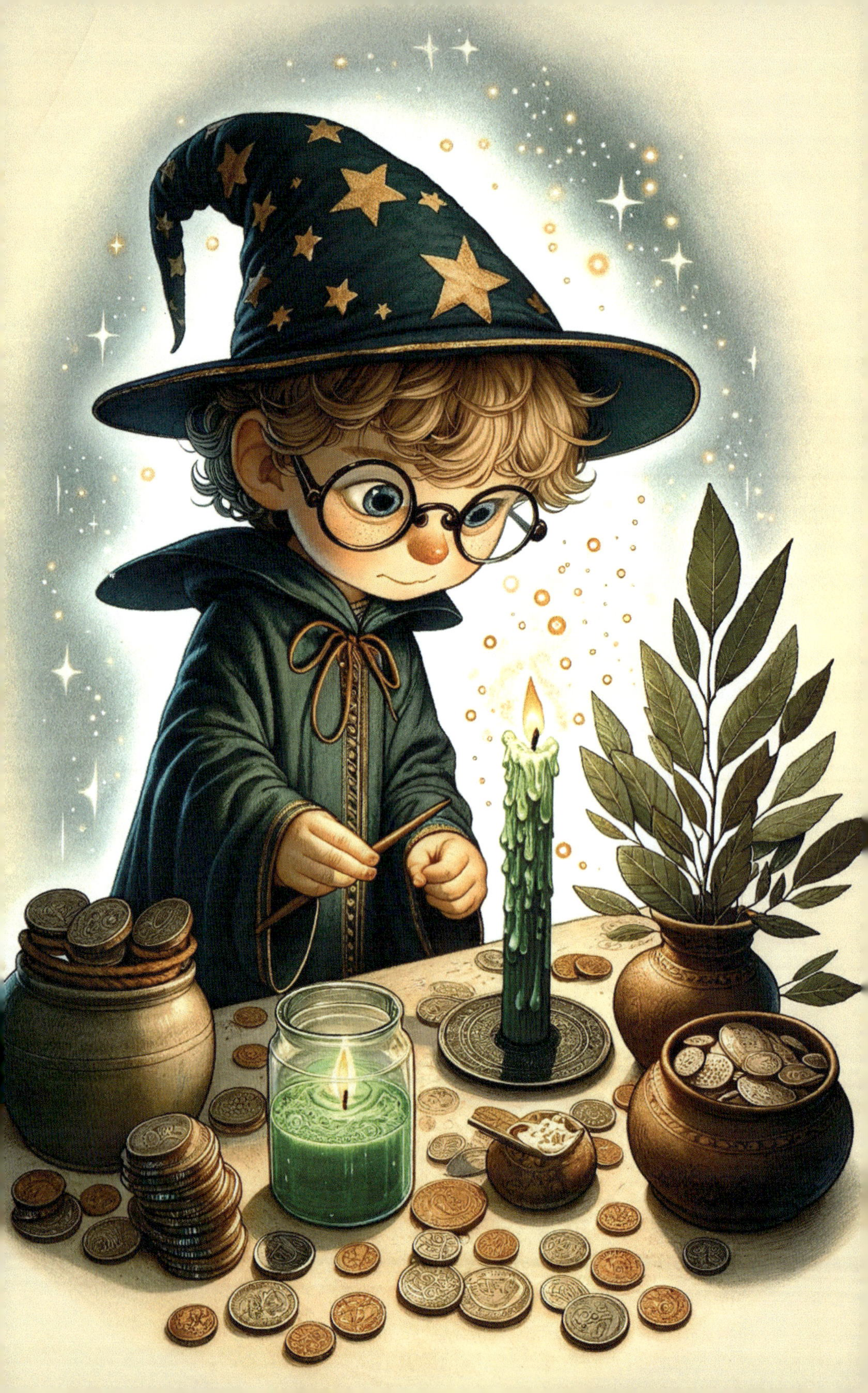

Prosperity Spell

Purpose: To focus on attracting wealth, abundance, and financial success.

Magical Ingredients:
- A Green Candle - Green is the color of prosperity and wealth.
- Three Coins of Any Denomination - Symbolize the wealth you wish to attract.
- A Small Pot of Soil - Represents growth and the nurturing of financial goals.
- Bay Leaves - Traditionally associated with wealth and success.

Directions:
- Prepare Your Space: Find a quiet area where you can concentrate without interruption. Lay out your magical ingredients.
- Light the Candle: Light the green candle, visualizing its flame as the energy of wealth and prosperity.
- Place the Coins: Put the three coins around the base of the candle. As you place each coin, think of a financial goal or aspect of wealth you wish to attract.
- Pot of Soil: Place the pot of soil in front of the candle. This symbolizes the fertile ground for your financial growth.
- Add Bay Leaves: Place bay leaves in the soil. Each leaf represents a specific aspect of financial success or abundance you are seeking.
- Focus on your financial goals and recite the magical chant:

> "Candle burn and coins of three,
> Bring forth wealth and prosperity.
> Bay in soil, growth begin,
> Abundance flow from within."

- Visualize Success: Close your eyes and imagine your financial goals being met. See yourself thriving and prospering.
- Conclude the Ritual: Blow out the candle, affirming your commitment to your financial goals. Keep the coins in a wallet or purse as a reminder of your intention to attract wealth.

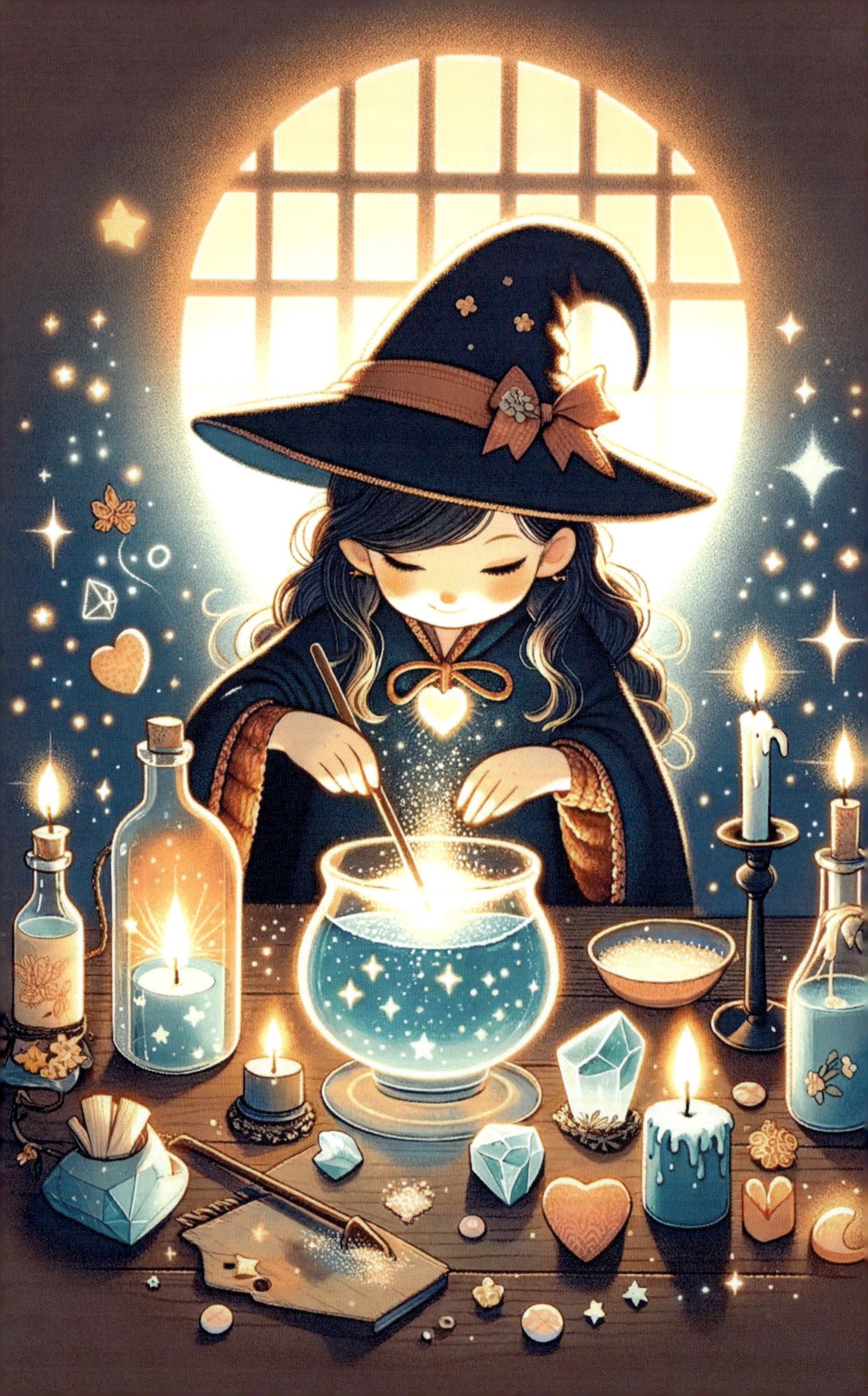

Healing Light Spell

Purpose: To help someone to feel better when they've been ill.

Magical Ingredients:
- A Blue Candle - Blue is associated with healing, calmness, and well-being.
- A Small Bunch of Fresh Herbs or Green Leaves - Symbolize vitality and the rejuvenation of nature. Herbs like mint or rosemary are good choices.
- A Clear Quartz Crystal - Believed to amplify healing energy and positive intentions.
- A Glass of Water - Represents clarity, purity, and the essence of life.

Directions:
- Prepare Your Space: Find a quiet, comfortable place where you can relax undisturbed. Lay out your magical ingredients gently.
- Light the Candle: Light the blue candle, envisioning its flame as a source of soothing, healing energy.
- Arrange the Herbs/Green Leaves: Place the herbs or leaves around the candle. As you do, think about their natural vitality and healing properties.
- Set the Crystal: Place the clear quartz crystal near the candle to amplify your healing intentions.
- Place the Glass of Water: Set the glass of water close to the candle, symbolizing the cleansing and renewing power of water.
- With a calm and hopeful spirit, recite the healing chant:

> "Candle blue, burn so bright,
> Ease my body, day and night.
> Herbs and crystal, healing light,
> Restore my strength, with all your might."

- Visualize Healing: Close your eyes and imagine the candle's light spreading through your body, bringing warmth, comfort, and healing to every part.
- Drink the Water: Slowly sip the glass of water, imagining it as a healing elixir revitalizing your body.

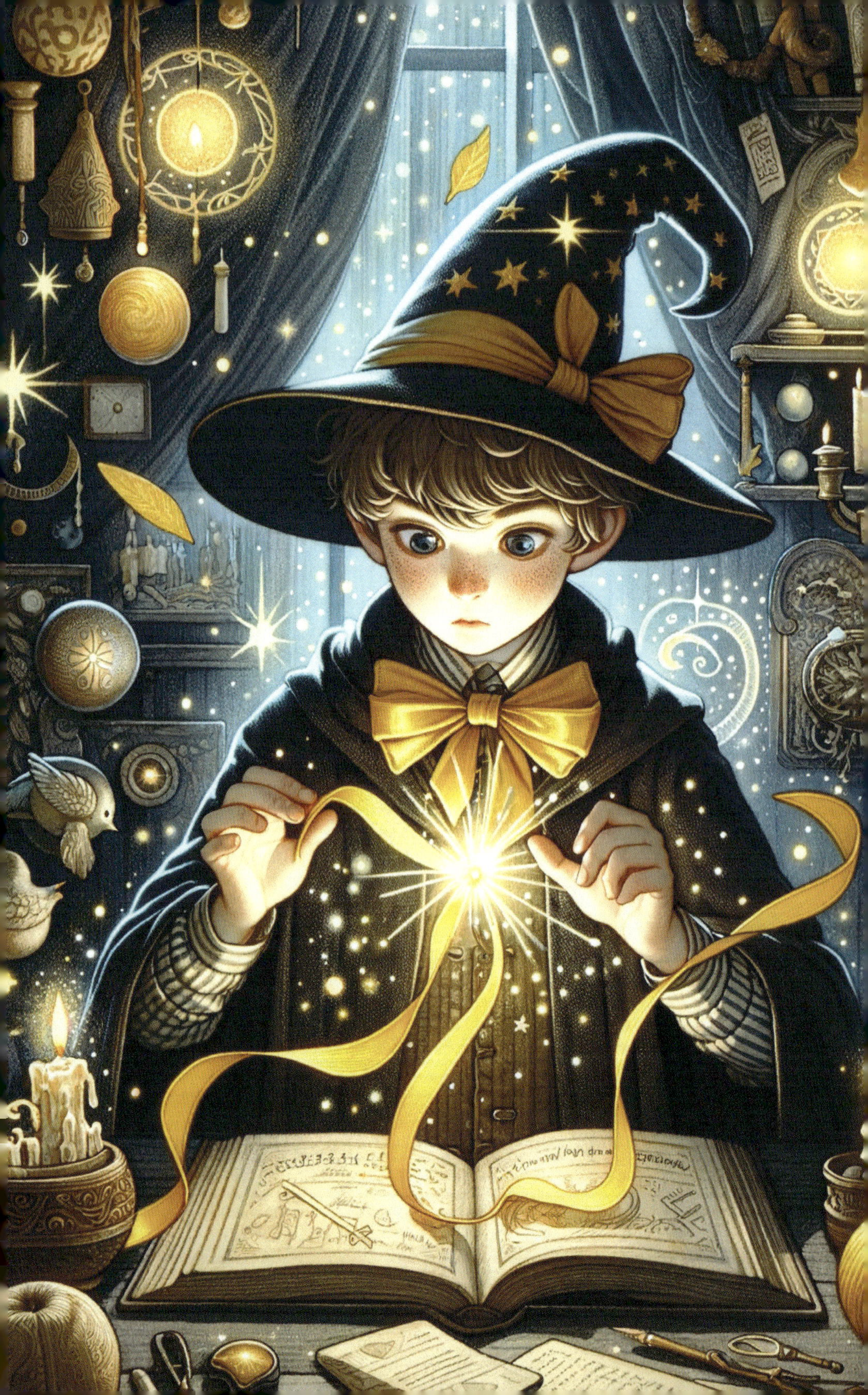

Create a Lucky Charm

Purpose: To charge an object with positive energy and good luck.

Magical Ingredients:
- A Small Object to Imbue with Luck - This could be a piece of jewelry, a keychain, a stone, or any small item you carry regularly.
- A Green Candle - Green symbolizes luck, growth, and prosperity.
- A Sprig of Clover or a Bay Leaf - Traditional symbols of good fortune.
- A Piece of Gold or Yellow Ribbon - Represents success and positive energy.

Directions:
- Prepare Your Space: Find a peaceful area where you can concentrate without distractions. Arrange your magical ingredients in front of you.
- Light the Candle: Light the green candle, visualizing its flame as a beacon of luck and good fortune.
- Place the Object: Set the item you wish to imbue with luck next to the candle.
- Add the Clover/Bay Leaf: Place the sprig of clover or bay leaf beside the object, lending it the essence of luck.
- Tie the Ribbon: Wrap the gold or yellow ribbon around the object (or simply place it nearby if it can't be tied), imagining it attracting positive energy.
- Focus on the object and your wish for good luck, and recite the magical chant:

> "Candle green and ribbon bright,
> Bring good fortune, day and night.
> With clover's touch and golden glow,
> Into this object, luck shall flow."

- Visualize the Luck: Close your eyes and imagine the object glowing with a warm, golden light, signifying it's now filled with luck and positive energy.
- Carry the Luck: Extinguish the candle and carry the object with you, or place it where you will see it often, as a reminder of the luck and positivity it now holds.

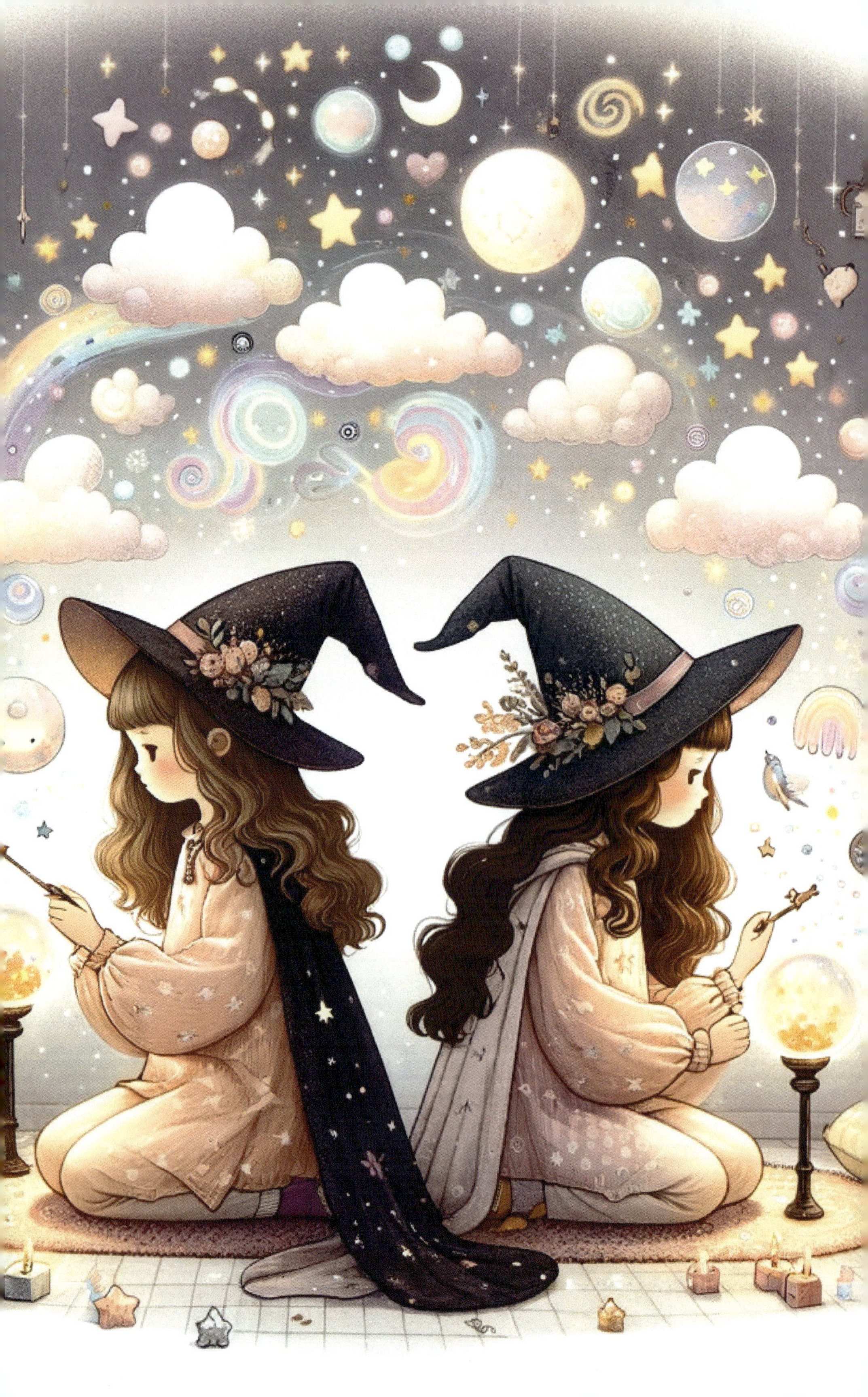

Starlight Sleepover Spell

Purpose: To create a magical atmosphere for a sleepover, ensuring a night of sweet dreams and cozy sleep.

Magical Ingredients:
Glow-in-the-Dark Stars - To create a starry night sky indoors.
A Small Pillow - Symbolizes comfort and relaxation.
A Soft Blanket - Represents warmth and security.

Directions:
- Prepare Your Sleepover Space: Set up your sleeping area with the pillow and blanket. Make it as cozy and inviting as possible.
- Create a Starry Sky: Stick the glow-in-the-dark stars on the ceiling or walls around your sleepover area, arranging them in fun patterns or constellations.
- Place the Pillow and Blanket: Position your pillow and blanket under the glow of the stars, making a snug nest for your sleep.
- As you settle into your sleepover spot, recite the magical chant with a whisper of excitement:

> "Stars that twinkle, stars that glow,
> Guard our sleepover, high and low.
> Pillow soft and blanket snug,
> Into dreams, we gently tug."

- Enjoy the Magical Atmosphere: Lie down and watch the stars gently glow in the dark, feeling the magical atmosphere around you.
- Drift into Sweet Dreams: Let the spell guide you into a peaceful and dream-filled sleep, surrounded by the gentle protection of the starlight.
- Awaken Refreshed: When you wake up from your sleepover, feel the joy and comfort of a night spent under the magical stars.

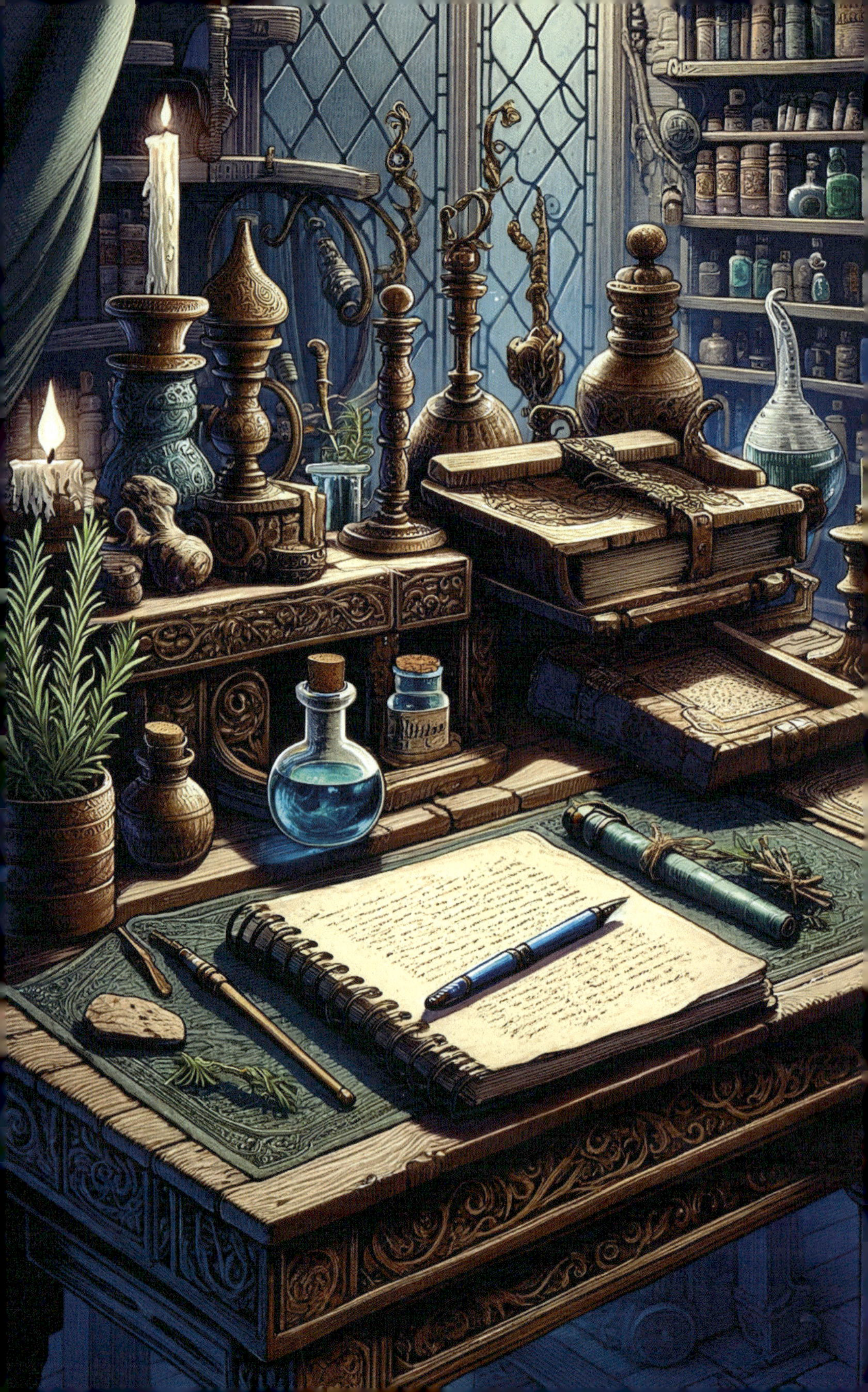

Memory Spell

Purpose: To assist in the retention and recall of information, perfect for studying or learning new skills.

Magical Ingredients:
- A Notepad - Symbolizes the gathering and holding of knowledge.
- A Blue Pen - Blue is often associated with clarity and intellectual energy.
- A Sprig of Rosemary - Traditionally linked to memory and clarity of thought.

Directions:
- Prepare Your Study Space: Find a quiet, comfortable place where you can concentrate. Arrange your notepad, blue pen, and sprig of rosemary neatly in front of you.
- Place the Rosemary: Lay the sprig of rosemary on top of your notepad, allowing its scent and symbolism to infuse your study materials with the essence of memory and focus.
- Pick up the Pen: Hold the blue pen in your hand, feeling ready and open to absorb information.
- With a clear mind and a steady voice, recite the magical chant:

    "Pen of blue and paper white,
    Rosemary, bring insight.
    Memory sharp, mind so keen,
    Recall the things I've heard and seen."

- Visualize Successful Learning: Close your eyes briefly and envision yourself absorbing information easily, recalling it effortlessly when needed.
- Begin Your Study Session: Open your notepad and start writing or studying, feeling empowered by the spell's intent.
- Close the Spell: After your study session, thank the rosemary for its aid and store your materials in a safe place, ready for your next learning adventure.

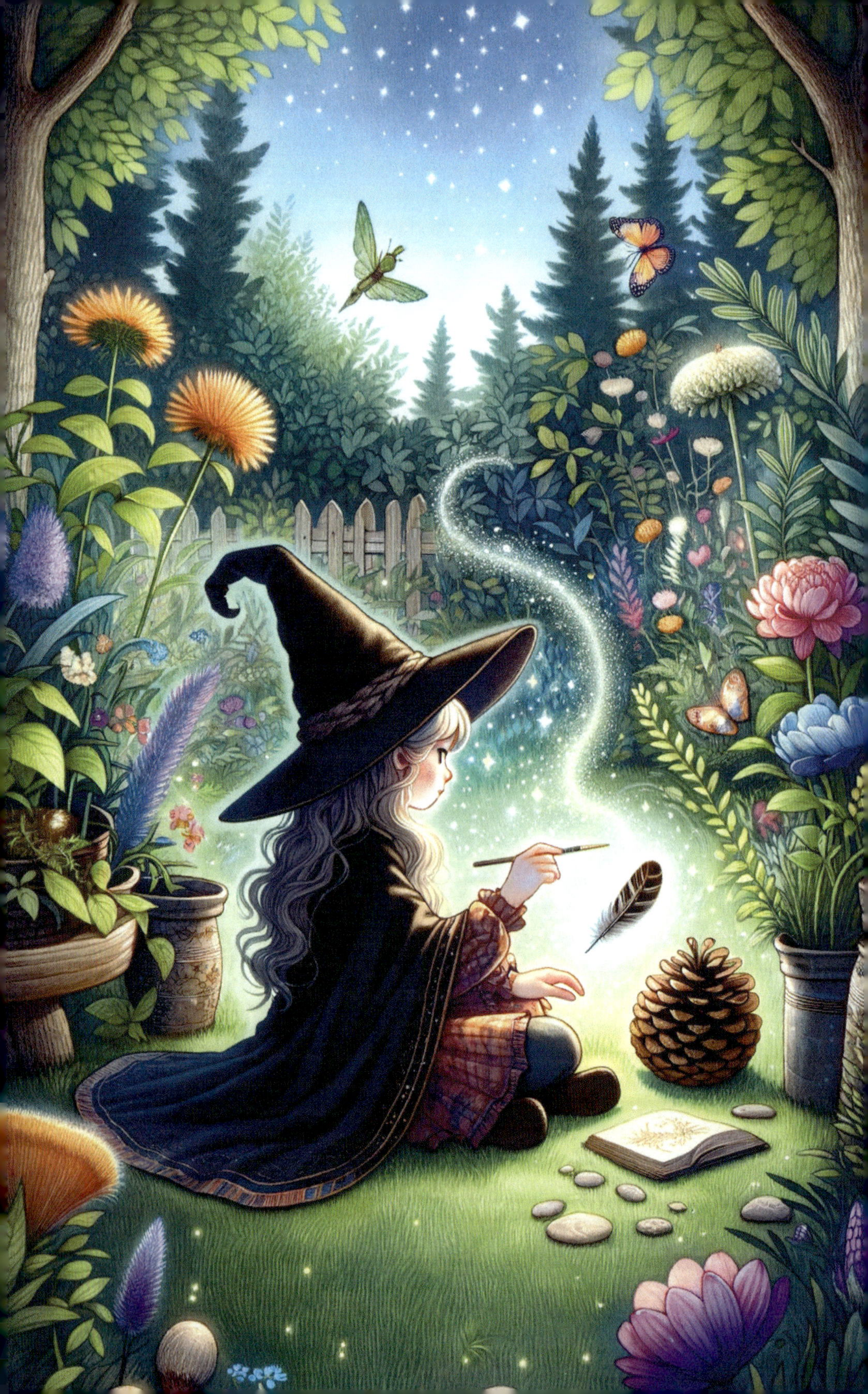

Weather Prediction Charm

Purpose: To spot the signs and predict the weather, engaging with nature in a whimsical way.

Magical Ingredients:
- A Pine Cone - A natural barometer, pine cones open and close depending on the humidity.
- A Feather - Represents the air and the wind.
- A Small Cup of Water - Symbolizes rain and moisture in the air.

Directions:
- Prepare Your Weather Station: Find a spot near a window or outdoors where you can observe the sky. Arrange your pine cone, feather, and cup of water on a flat surface.
- Observe the Pine Cone: Look at the pine cone. Pine cones tend to close when the air is humid (often before rain) and open in dry conditions.
- Feel the Feather: Hold the feather lightly in your hand. Its movement can give clues about the wind - if it's still, the air is calm; if it moves, there may be a breeze.
- Check the Water: Look at the surface of the water in the cup. Calm water may indicate clear weather, while ripples could suggest wind or changes coming.
- As you observe your natural weather tools, recite the magical chant:

> "Feather light and pine cone tight,
> Show us the weather, clear and bright.
> Water still, air so fair,
> Tell us what we might wear."

- Make Your Prediction: Based on your observations and the 'signs' from your magical ingredients, make a playful prediction about the weather.
- Embrace Nature's Surprise: Remember, the weather can be unpredictable, and this charm is all about the fun of guessing and observing, not about accurate forecasts.

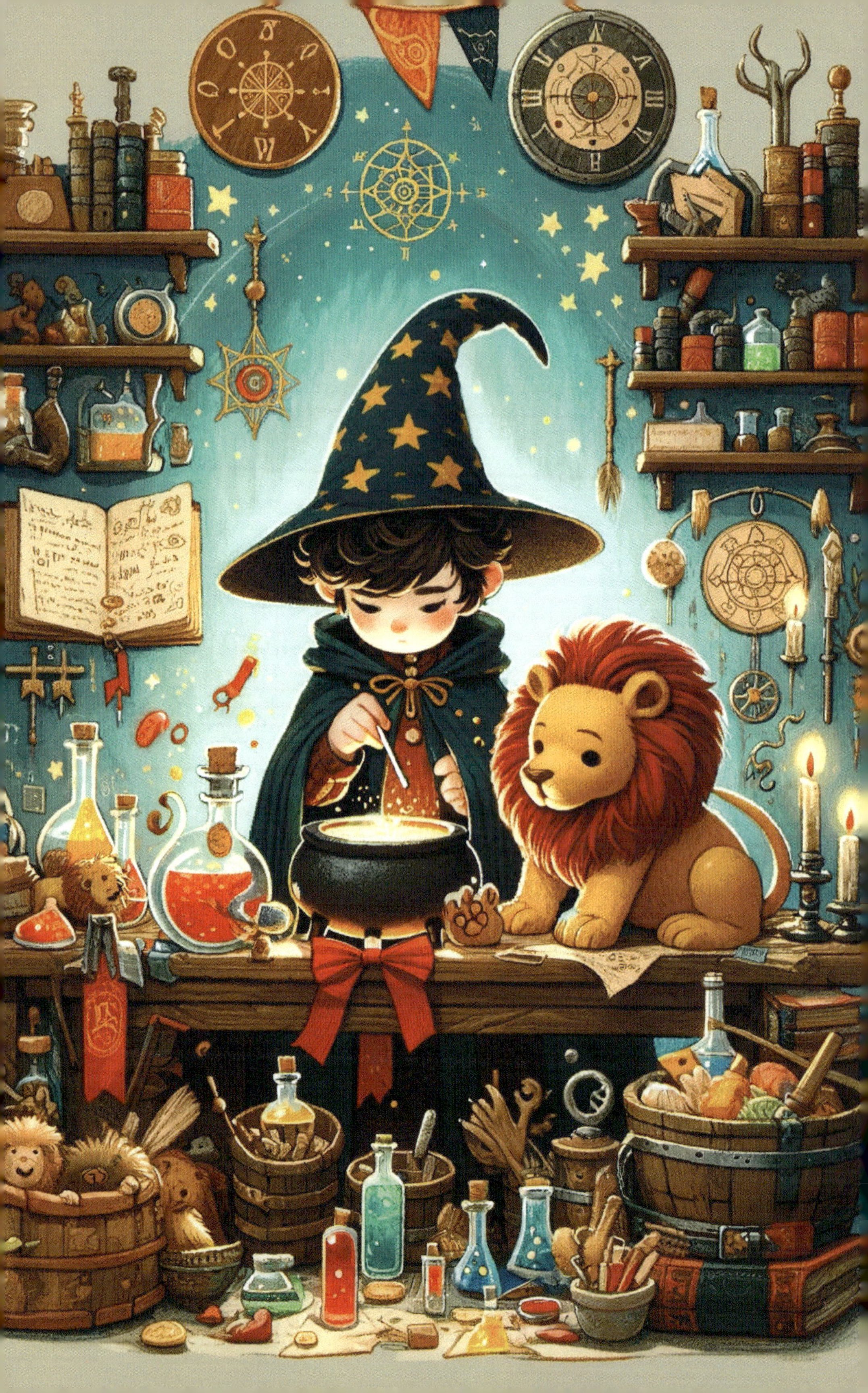

Courage Spell

Purpose: To inspire courage and bravery in new or challenging situations.

Magical Ingredients:
A Toy Lion - Represents courage, strength, and bravery.
A Red Scarf or Ribbon - Red symbolizes courage and boldness.
A Small Bell - Its sound is believed to dispel fear and bring clarity.

Directions:
- Prepare Your Brave Space: Find a comfortable area where you feel strong and undisturbed. Place the toy lion in front of you.
- Drape the Red Scarf or Ribbon: Wrap the red scarf or ribbon around the toy lion, symbolizing the wrapping of courage around yourself.
- Ring the Bell: Gently ring the small bell three times. Each ring symbolizes the awakening of courage, the clearing of fear, and the strengthening of resolve.
- Stand tall, facing the toy lion, and recite the magical chant with conviction:

    "Lion strong and scarf of red,
    Bring courage to my heart and head.
    Ring the bell, let fear dispel,
    In bravery's light, I shall dwell."

- Visualize Courage Filling You: Imagine the sound of the bell filling you with confidence. Picture yourself standing as tall and proud as the lion, filled with bravery.
- Embrace the Courage: Feel the imaginary strength and courage from the lion transferring to you, making you ready to face any challenges.
- Carry the Courage Forward: Keep the toy lion or the red scarf or ribbon with you, especially when you need a little extra courage.

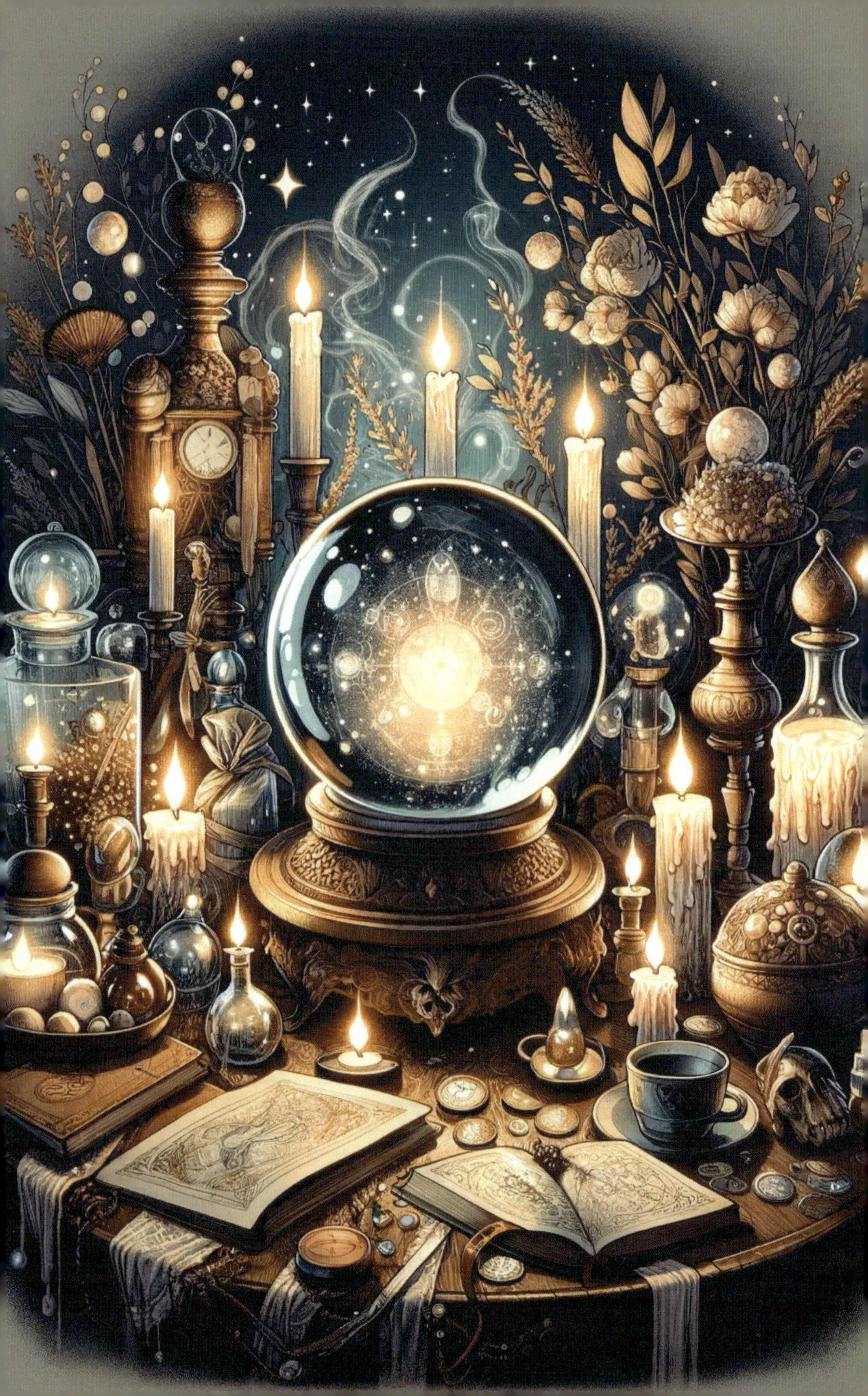

Divination Spell

Purpose: To symbolically peer into the future and unlock the mysteries of tomorrow, using a crystal ball as a focal point for imagination and insight.

Magical Ingredients:
- A Crystal Ball or Glass Globe - Represents the window to the future and the realm of possibilities.
- A Circle of Candles - To illuminate the path ahead and clear the mind for visions. LED candles can be used for safety.
- A Velvet Cloth or Dark Fabric - To create a serene environment and focus energies.
- A Sprig of Rosemary - Associated with memory and clarity of thought.

Directions:
- Prepare Your Space: Find a peaceful area where you won't be disturbed. Drape the velvet cloth or dark fabric on a table and place the crystal ball in the center.
- Arrange the Candles: Carefully place candles in a circle around the crystal ball, ensuring they're at a safe distance to prevent any hazard.
- Add the Rosemary: Lay the sprig of rosemary beside the crystal ball to enhance clarity and focus.
- Light the Candles: Illuminate the candles one by one, focusing on the flame's ability to light the way to future insights.
- With your hands gently placed around the crystal ball, recite the magical chant:

> "Orb of crystal, clear and bright,
> Show the future in your light.
> Rosemary for clarity, candle's glow to see,
> Reveal what might, one day, be."

- Gaze into the Crystal Ball: Look deeply into the crystal ball, allowing your eyes to relax and your mind to open. Let your imagination flow freely, exploring possible futures.
- Reflect on the Experience: Take a moment to contemplate any thoughts, images, or feelings that arose during your gazing. Write them down if you wish.
- Close the Ritual: Extinguish the candles safely, thanking the crystal ball for its 'insights'. Fold the cloth and store your items respectfully.

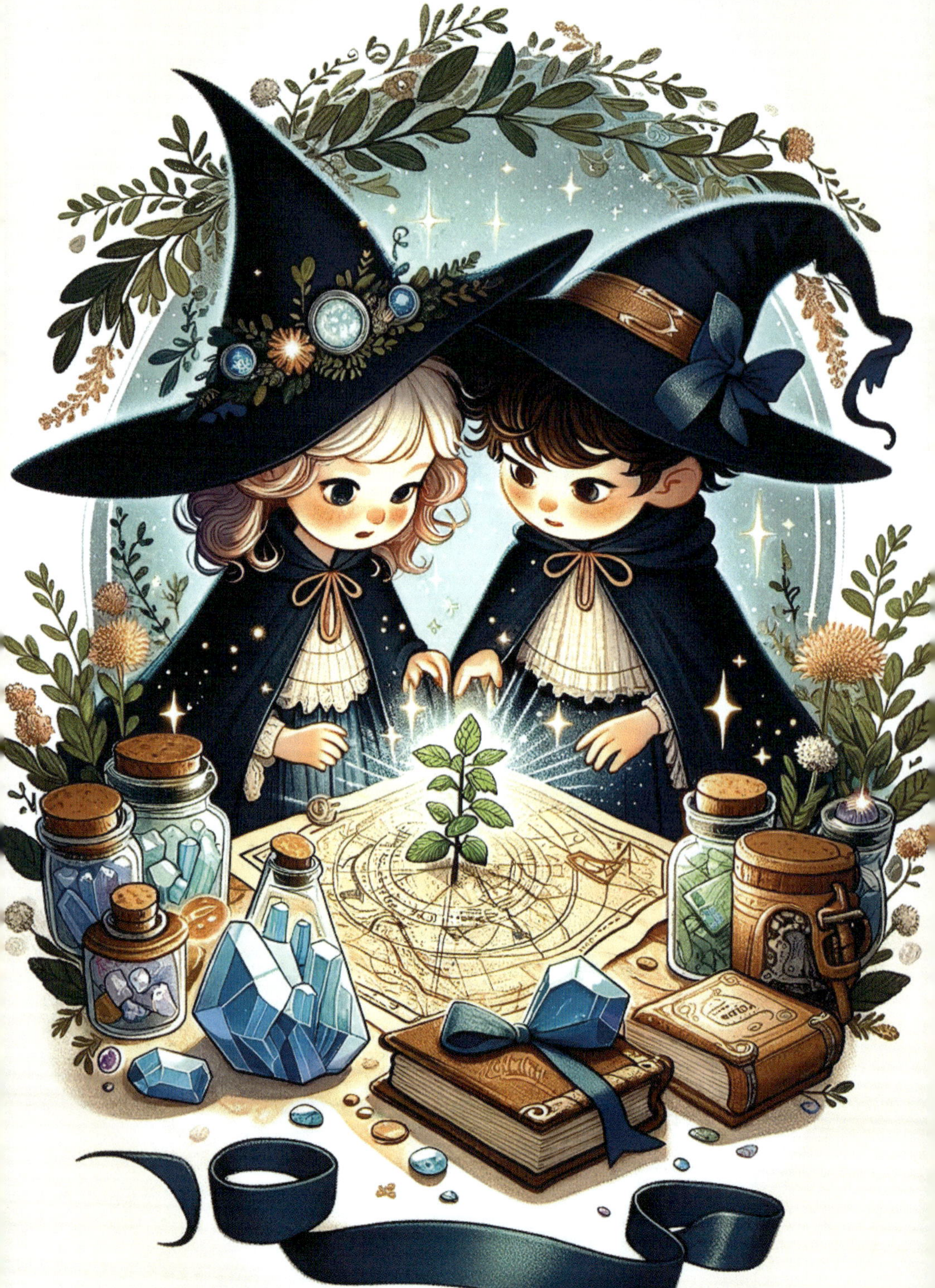

Tranquil Travel Spell

Purpose: To promote a safe, smooth, and enjoyable journey, whether traveling near or far.

Magical Ingredients:
- A Small Map or Representation of Your Destination - Symbolizes the journey ahead.
- A Small Stone or Crystal - Represents grounding and protection during travel.
- A Blue Ribbon or String - Blue for calmness and safe passage.
- A Sprig of Mint or Lavender - For a refreshing and calming presence on your journey.

Directions:
- Prepare Your Space: Prior to your journey, find a quiet place where you can sit undisturbed. Lay out your magical ingredients.
- Place the Map: Set the map or representation of your destination in front of you, visualizing the path you will take.
- Add the Stone/Crystal: Place the stone or crystal on the map, symbolizing stability and protection throughout your travels.
- Tie the Blue Ribbon: Attach the blue ribbon or string to the stone or crystal, invoking feelings of calm and safety.
- Add the Herb: Place the sprig of mint or lavender with your travel talismans to bring a sense of freshness and ease to your journey.
- Focus on your upcoming journey, holding the stone or crystal, and recite the magical chant:

> "Map to guide and stone to guard,
> Blue ribbon, protect from hard.
> Mint refresh, lavender calm,
> Ensure my journey without qualm."

- Visualize the Journey: Close your eyes and imagine your journey unfolding smoothly, with each step or mile bringing you closer to your destination in safety and joy.
- Carry Your Talismans: Keep these items with you during your travels as a reminder of your intentions and the protective spell you've cast.

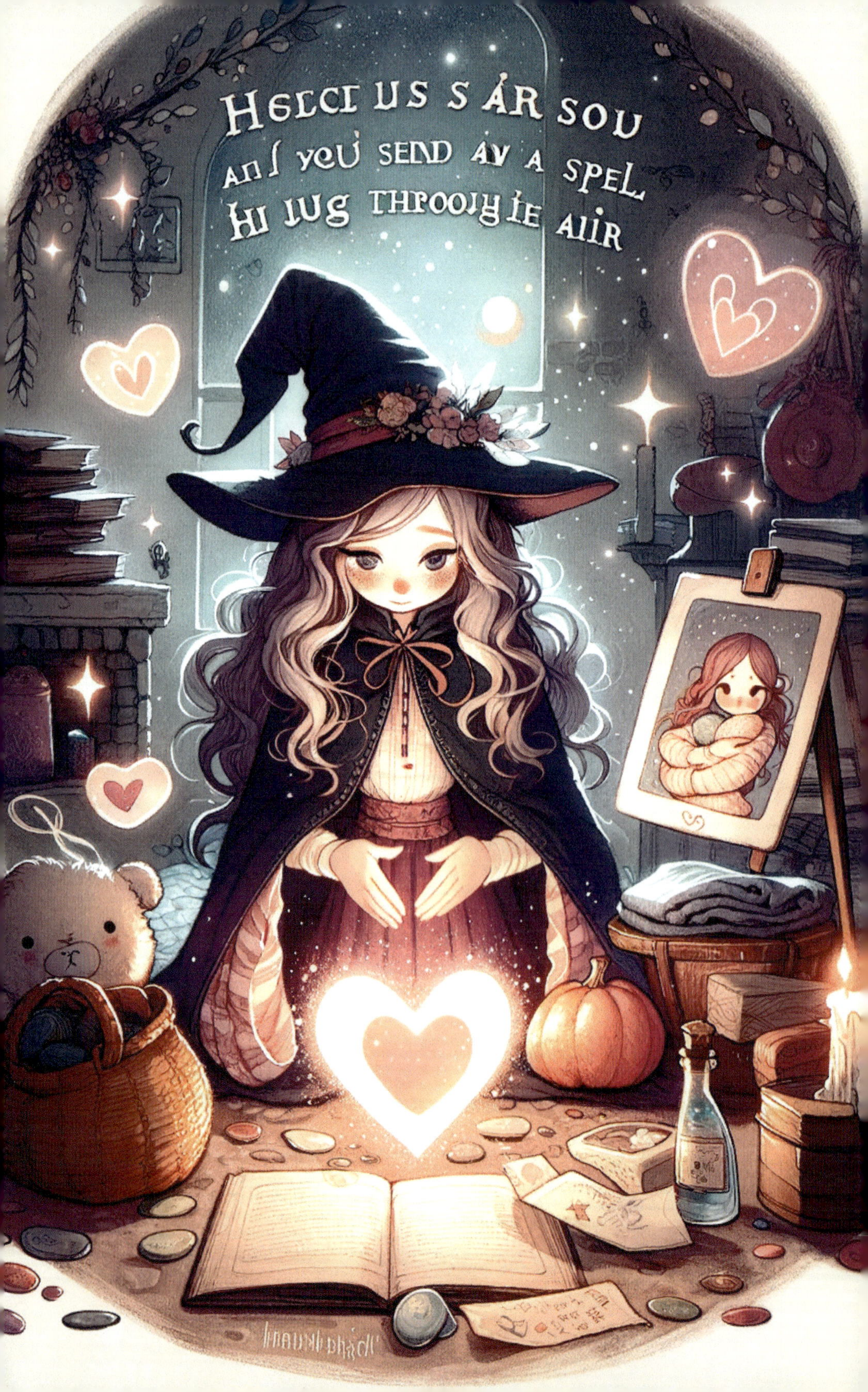
HELCI US S ÁR SOU
AN/ YOU SEND AV A SPEL
HI LUG THROOJYIE AIR

Distant Hug Spell

Purpose: To send a comforting, loving hug to a friend or relative who is not physically present.

Magical Ingredients:
- A Cozy Scarf or Piece of Fabric - Symbolizes the warmth and comfort of a hug.
- A Picture or Drawing of the Person - To focus your thoughts and love on them.
- Two Small Stones - Representing you and the person you're sending the hug to.
- A Heart-Shaped Object - Symbolizes the love and affection you're sending.

Directions:
- Prepare Your Space: Find a peaceful spot where you can sit comfortably and think of your loved one. Lay out the scarf or fabric.
- Place the Picture and Stones: Set the picture or drawing of your friend or relative on the fabric. Place one stone to represent you and the other to represent them, on either side of the picture.
- Add the Heart: Place the heart-shaped object between the two stones, creating a connection of love.
- Recite the Chant: Hold your hands over the heart-shaped object, close your eyes, and focus on sending a hug:

> "Heart to heart and hand in hand,
> Across the miles, through air and land.
> My hug to you, on wings of love,
> Embracing tight, from me to you above."

- Visualize the Hug: Imagine a warm, loving hug enveloping your friend or relative. Feel the love and comfort you're sending across the distance.
- Seal the Spell: Gently fold the fabric around the picture, stones, and heart, symbolizing the completion and delivery of your hug.
- Carry the Warmth: Keep the fabric bundle in a safe place as a symbol of the ongoing connection and love between you and your distant loved one.

Riddle Me This

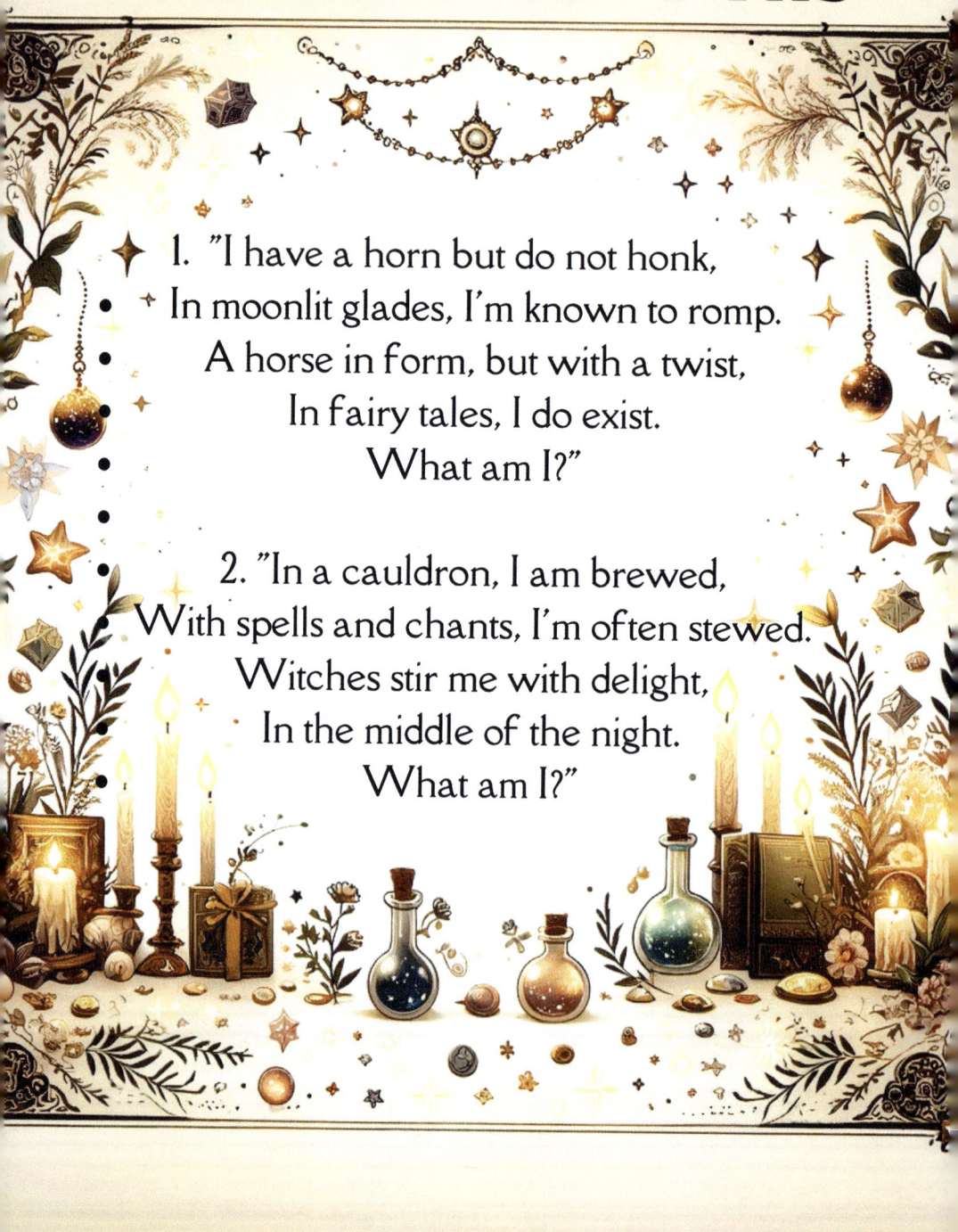

1. "I have a horn but do not honk,
In moonlit glades, I'm known to romp.
A horse in form, but with a twist,
In fairy tales, I do exist.
What am I?"

2. "In a cauldron, I am brewed,
With spells and chants, I'm often stewed.
Witches stir me with delight,
In the middle of the night.
What am I?"

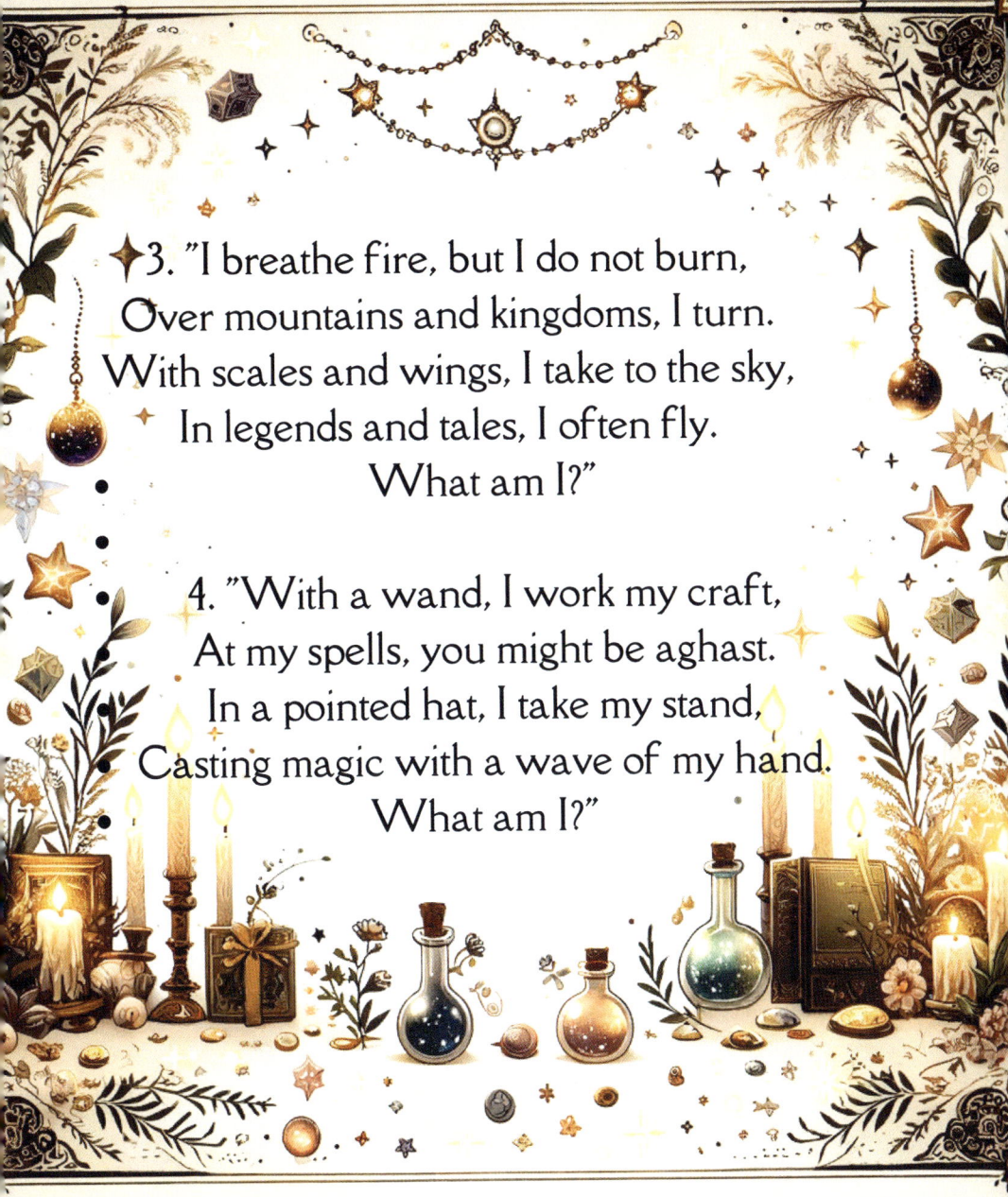

Riddle Me That

3. "I breathe fire, but I do not burn,
Over mountains and kingdoms, I turn.
With scales and wings, I take to the sky,
In legends and tales, I often fly.
What am I?"

4. "With a wand, I work my craft,
At my spells, you might be aghast.
In a pointed hat, I take my stand,
Casting magic with a wave of my hand.
What am I?"

Answer: 1. Unicorn 2. A Potion 3. Dragon 4. A witch or wizard

Blessed Be

Printed in Great Britain
by Amazon